Hermine, an Empress in Exile

The untold story of the Kaiser's second wife

Hermine:
an Empress in Exile

The untold story of the
Kaiser's second wife

Moniek Bloks

Winchester, UK
Washington, USA

First published by Chronos Books, 2020
Chronos Books is an imprint of John Hunt Publishing Ltd., No. 3 East St., Alresford,
Hampshire SO24 9EE, UK
office@jhpbooks.com
www.johnhuntpublishing.com
www.chronosbooks.com

For distributor details and how to order please visit the 'Ordering' section on our website.

Text copyright: Moniek Bloks 2019

ISBN: 978 1 78904 478 2
978 1 78904 479 9 (ebook)
Library of Congress Control Number: 2019948219

A CIP catalogue record for this book is available from the British Library.

Design: Stuart Davies

UK: Printed and bound by CPI Group (UK) Ltd, Croydon, CR0 4YY
US: Printed and bound by Thomson-Shore, 7300 West Joy Road, Dexter, MI 48130

We operate a distinctive and ethical publishing philosophy in
all areas of our business, from our global network of authors to
production and worldwide distribution.

Contents

With special thanks to my Patreon patrons for their continued support, especially Emmalisa.

Introduction

On 22 February 1933, guests gathered in the von Dirksen house in the Margrethenstrasse in Berlin. Ten minutes after eight, Hermine – the would-be Empress of Germany and Queen of Prussia – appeared. She was expecting to meet a very important man by the name of Adolf Hitler, but Mr. Hitler was not there yet. The beautiful 17th century English clock struck the quarter of an hour – then the half hour. Was he not coming?

At a quarter to nine, Hitler entered the room without a word of apology. Frau von Dirksen was now faced with a difficult protocol question: Should she introduce the Empress to the Chancellor or the Chancellor to the Empress? Hitler solved the problem for her. He stepped elegantly up to Hermine, clicked the heels of his shoes, bowed stiffly and said: "Hitler!"

"Heil Hitler! Mr. Hitler!" Hermine replied nervously as the Führer gallantly kissed her hand. During the following meal, Hermine had no opportunity to speak to Hitler herself or for her cause – the restoration of her husband, the exiled Emperor Wilhelm II of Germany. The two sat at opposite ends of the table.

At last, she was able to speak to him after dinner. Would he be willing to reintroduce the monarchy, or at least allow the Emperor to return to Germany? "I would be proud if I could contribute something to the return of your noble family to their legally appropriate place," said Hitler. "No one is more aware of the great merit that the House of Hohenzollern has acquired for the Fatherland, but unfortunately the time is not ripe, in the present moment such a measure will provoke only unrest and turmoil, this attitude we have to take into account in our delicate situation today, has by no means welcomed a sweep of this kind. I can tell Your Imperial Majesty in the strictest confidence that an exceptionally important English agent will inform me even before we have taken the government that the

1

English government has been most concerned about any attempt to reintroduce the monarchy in Germany."[1]

The monarchy was never restored in Germany, but it wasn't for lack of effort. Hermine, born Hermine Reuss of Greiz, the fifth child and fourth daughter of Heinrich XXII, Prince Reuss of Greiz and Princess Ida Mathilde Adelheid of Schaumburg-Lippe, probably never imagined she would one day marry the exiled Emperor of Germany and would promote his return to power to one of the most evil men in history, Adolf Hitler.

Her youth was overshadowed by her brother's illness and the early death of her mother. Her first marriage to Prince Johann Georg of Schönaich-Carolath brought her five children but her husband's long illness meant that she was more his nurse than his wife. When he died of tuberculosis in 1920, Hermine vowed never to marry again. Hermine wrote in her memoirs, "I was strongly determined never to marry again, never to surrender the precious right to be the master of my soul."[2]

Things changed shortly before Easter 1922 when her young son Prince Georg Wilhelm asked her if he could write a letter to the former Emperor of Germany, who had been in exile in the Netherlands since his abdication in 1918 and whose wife Auguste Viktoria had just passed away. The young Prince told his mother that he wanted to fight for the Emperor when he became a man. He wrote to the Emperor, "I am sorry because you are so terribly lonely." Hermine posted the letter and was surprised to find both of them invited to the Emperor's exile in Doorn. In the end, Hermine went alone to Doorn as she did not want to interrupt her son's education and it became her first visit to a house that would become her home for the next 20 years.

The 63-year-old Wilhelm soon proposed to the 34-year-old Hermine, much to the horror and shock of his family. However, he refused to back down and the two were married later that year at Doorn. The Emperor was not allowed to go to Germany, but Hermine was. She often visited her first husband's estates in Silesia and when she was in Berlin, she was given the use of apartments in the Old Palace.

With the rise of National Socialism and Adolf Hitler, Hermine saw an opportunity for her to become more than an Empress in name. She wanted the restoration of her husband and encouraged the attention of Hermann Göring – a powerful figure in the Nazi party – who came to Doorn twice. In her meetings with Hitler, he gave her hope and he sometimes promised that he wanted the monarchy to return only to say that the time just wasn't right. The German invasion of the Netherlands saw the Emperor welcome the German troops with open arms, but his death just a year later put an end to any rumours of a restoration.

Hermine would survive her husband for just six years. After the Emperor's death, she returned to Silesia where she was eventually forced to flee from the violence of war. At the end of the war, she was arrested and taken to Frankfurt an der Oder where she seemed to age overnight, and she died under mysterious circumstances. In a twist of fate, Wilhelm lies buried on the Doorn estate – not wishing to return to Germany without the restoration of the monarchy – while Hermine lies with her husband's first wife and several of her stepsons in the Antique Temple in Potsdam.

By the end of the war, she was completely disillusioned, asking herself, "What kind of misfortune has that man brought over our people?"[2]

Chapter 1

Princess Hermine

Princess Hermine Reuss of Greiz (elder line) was born on 17 December 1887 as the daughter of Heinrich XXII, Prince Reuss of Greiz and Princess Ida Mathilde Adelheid of Schaumburg-Lippe. The small principality of Reuss-Greiz in Germany had been ruled by her father since 1859. The family also had a so-called Younger or Junior Line, which ruled over the Principality of Reuss-Gera. Unusually all male members of the family carried the name Heinrich and a numbering sequence in order of their births. While the Younger line began a new sequence every century, the Elder line numbered to 100 and then began anew.

She was their fifth child and fourth daughter. The disappointment in her gender was great but as Hermine herself said in her memoirs, "They were disappointed in my sex, not in me."[1] Hermine vividly described the events of her birth in her memoir, though she does not mention where she heard the story. Her father paced in front of the door to the room where his wife Ida was in labour. Every once in a while, a servant went into the room and came back to inform him, "Not yet, Highness, not yet!" Both parents prayed for a boy.[2] Upon being informed that the child was a girl, her father hid his feelings and comforted her disappointed mother. Her elder brother, also named Heinrich, had been the only boy born to her parents so far, but he had suffered a "ghastly, almost incomprehensible"[3] accident in his childhood, which had rendered him mentally and physically disabled. The accident itself began as a medical procedure. As a child, Heinrich had a squint that was caused by a slight contraction of the optic nerve. The doctors decided to correct the problem but had difficulty subduing the child. He was dragged into the operating room and was held down, but he renewed his struggle just as the knife was poised over his eye. He suffered a brain injury, although the exact nature of which was never determined.[4]

Her baptism took place on 5 January 1888, but her mother was not yet strong enough to participate. Water from the river Jordan was used to baptise the infant Hermine. Her godparents were her grandmother, Princess Hermine of Schaumburg-Lippe (born of Waldeck and Pyrmont), the widowed Duchess Mathilde of Schleswig-Holstein[5], Countess Auguste of Stolberg-Stolberg, her grandfather Adolf I, Prince of Schaumburg-Lippe and Prince Wilhelm of Schaumburg-Lippe. Out of the ordinary for the time, she received just one name, Hermine.[6]

Four years later, her mother gave birth to another girl, named for her, and died shortly after of complications. Hermine remembered her mother only on her deathbed as she was just four years old when she died. In her memoirs, she described hushed voices, a dark room and the pale roses that covered her bed.[7] The younger Hermine inherited her mother's love of reading and remembered her library being lined with books in several languages.[8] She grew up revering the memory of her mother and the room in which Princess Ida died remained untouched. Hermine spoke highly of her father in her memoirs but described him as a broken man after Princess Ida's death. He withdrew from public life and became even more isolated by his increasing deafness.

An undated letter from Hermine to her father has survived and judging by the text it is probably from her early childhood, "Dear father, I love you so very much. Oh, how many beautiful things you give me. So much! The clothes, everything, everything! It's so much. And I give you nothing, only something for Christmas or your birthday. And you give me so many wonderful things. So many stones and goats! I hope that you will be healthy for ever. Oh, how wonderful that would be. Dear father, dear father, you are so very good. I love you so much! Oh yes, Your wicked daughter Hermine."[9]

Her childhood was not one of joy, mostly due to the circumstances surrounding her brother and the early death of her mother. She learned to speak German, English and French but lamented her lack of education in sports. Her father had never cared for sports and so she did not learn to ride a horse until later in life. She was close to her three elder sisters. Emma had been ten years old when Princess Ida died and tried to take on a mothering role, but eight-year-old Marie had been more suited for the role. She was especially close to Caroline, who was three years older than her. Hermine described Caroline as "our genius."[10] The young Princess Ida, who was a sickly child, was the spoiled darling of the family. The sisters were not close to their brother, whose condition made it difficult to communicate with them or even play games with them. Near the hunting lodge Ida-Waldhaus in Greiz, Hermine came in contact with ordinary women whose husbands worked in the forest. She shared coffee and wholewheat bread with them. "They did not treat me like a Princess, but like a poor motherless little girl. I learned more from them than I ever learned in school. I shared their lives and they opened their hearts to me."[11] Of her father she wrote, "A smile on his sad face was rewarding enough for us to finish the most difficult tasks."[12]

The family spent the winters at their father's residence in Greiz and the summers in the hunting lodge nearby. Summer vacations were spent in Castle Burgk on the Saale and Hermine was especially fond of Burgk. "There was no modern splendour at Schloss Burgk. The kitchen took up an entire wing and was covered with soot from over a century. The smoke blows freely through the kitchen. In winter the floor of the kitchen is often covered with snow, which was blown through the chimney and became black. It is a wonderful spectacle to see the black snow fall. Our governesses were most unmerciful when we threw these black snowballs as children."[13] In 1934, she sold her share in Schloss Burgk to her brother-in-law, Christoph Martin of Stolberg-Rossla and she was quite heartbroken when she wrote to administrator Merkel, "It had to be for my children, who after my death, would be half owners. They have a beloved home in Saabor where they are the sole owners and have a place. That's how I made this heavy sacrifice, since I could not maintain both."[14]

The young Hermine had been fascinated by the skeleton of a large hunting dog that had been buried alive in the wall over the gate of the castle. It had been discovered 300 years later with a huge key with three crosses between its paws. Supposedly, to immure a living creature was to bring luck. In a nearby castle, a child had been immured alive.[15]

As a child, she met her future stepdaughter Cecilie of Mecklenburg-Schwerin, who was then but 10 years old. They would not meet again until 16 years later.[16]

At the age of 14, Hermine lost her father as well. He had come back to Reuss in March against the advice of his doctors, who knew that it would be bad for his health. He was taken from the train on a stretcher on the day before his birthday, knowing that he may not see another one. He took a drive with the children that lasted over two hours and spent the next few days in bed. With his last bit of strength, he managed to visit the grave of Princess Ida. He died on 19 April 1902.

Hermine's disabled brother was now the reigning Prince. She described how he entered the room where their father lay and burst into convulsive tears before throwing himself upon the body of his father. It took hours to calm him down and then only with the aid of sedatives. The next day it was as though he had no recollection of what had happened.[17] For six weeks, every bell in Reuss tolled for one hour every day in memory of their father. In his last will, he had specified that there should be no public mourning to save his people the expense of purchasing mourning clothes.[18] One of the first messages of condolences came from the Kaiser and he sent his cousin Prince Friedrich Heinrich of Prussia to represent him at the funeral.[19]

Hermine had an early fascination with the man she was destined to marry, though she admitted to never once imagining that she would end up marrying him, realising all too well that rarely infatuations developed into mature love.[20] Strikingly, she wrote in her memoirs, "An empire had to fall before my dream came true."[21] It was her aunt Princess Marie Reuss of Greiz, who had married Count Friedrich of Ysenburg and Büdingen in 1875, who often came to visit and brought her niece photos and postcards of the man she idolised. "Ever since I was a child, the Emperor inspired my imagination. My aunt, who knew of my enthusiasm, helped to make my heart beat faster. She presented me with photos of the Emperor, sometimes a postcard or a coloured art print. My room was adorned with his pictures and my collection grew more and more. His face greeted me from every wall. He kept watch over my daytime school tasks and my dreams. The Emperor commanded a girlish imagination."[22]

On 3 April 1903, Hermine was confirmed in the City Church of Greiz. The Greizer newspaper reported, "With a loud and clear voice, Princess Hermine professed. It was a solemn moment. The whole celebration made a deep impression with its simplicity."[23] The day ended with a festive lunch and a gala in the evening.

She saw Emperor Wilhelm II of Germany for the first time during the wedding of her favourite sister Caroline to Wilhelm Ernst, Grand Duke of Saxe-Weimar on 30 April 1903 at Bückeburg Palace. Hermine was just 15 years old at the time and her sister only 19. Bückeburg Palace belonged to their guardian, their mother's older brother Georg, Prince of Schaumburg-Lippe. The wedding was celebrated there because the amount of guests expected could not be accommodated at Greiz, but the children knew the palace well and Hermine described it as their second home.[24] She remembered one figure distinctly looming over all the other guests, the Emperor.[25] Her uncle had promised to introduce her to the Emperor at the wedding, as her three older sisters had already met him at a hunting party and Hermine had been deemed too young then. She described how she curtseyed before the Emperor and wanted to run away. It was an unforgettable experience to her, but the Emperor paid little attention. To him, she was just the fourth daughter of a Prince and he was a monarch.[26] "How could he have foreseen that this blushing little girl was his future wife? I stood there frozen on the spot where the Emperor had received my greeting. The Emperor went on and chatted with my uncle."[27]

It was a splendid match for Caroline, but Hermine's sister was not happy. She hardly knew the man she was going to marry and abhorred the life that was waiting for her in Weimar.[28] But even the encouraging words of Queen Wilhelmina of the Netherlands could not ease the young bride's mind. The Emperor even spoke with the bridegroom, who also had his doubts, and said, "Only love can turn a palace into a home. Caroline is like a little bird, fallen out of its nest. She will miss the sisters who loved her. It will take her some time before she learns to be at home on the cold parquet floor of your castle."[29] The bridegroom retaliated, "The Princess Caroline has treated me badly, yes, insulted me, I simply cannot do it." The Emperor then raised his voice, "You have given me an Oath of Allegiance, and I order you to marry tomorrow."[30] The wedding went ahead as planned and just two weeks later Hermine's eldest sister Emma married Count Erich Kunigl von Ehrenburg. The two ceremonies could not have been more different and this time, it was a love match. Her father had reluctantly consented to the match shortly before his death and it was not made public until a year after his death. Hermine wrote that Emma never regretted her choice.[31]

The departure of two sisters made the other children lonely. Hermine missed her sisters terribly. Hermine and her sister Marie were invited by their new brother-in-law, the Grand Duke, to witness his entry into his capital. Caroline gave her sisters a tour of the palace, even pointing out to Hermine, the bookworm, the Green Chateau, which housed the library. After witnessing their sister's coronation, Hermine and her sisters Marie and Ida travelled to the Belgian seaside resort of Blankenberghe. Though they toured several Belgian cities, they never ventured into the Netherlands. Marie received an invitation from their sister Emma to come to them at Schloss Ehrenburg. While there, she met her future husband, Freiherr Ferdinand von Gnagnoni, whom she would marry in 1904. "She, too, preferred love to a coronet," wrote Hermine.[32]

Now just Hermine and Ida remained unmarried. Hermine divided her time between her sick brother and Caroline. But just two years after Caroline's wedding, tragedy struck the family once more. Caroline, who had already been unhappy with her match, did not fit into the rigid court of Weimar. Hermine wrote, "Incapable of hatred, incapable of complaining, she consumed herself. She could not thrive in an uncongenial atmosphere. The struggle with the environment killed her. The Grand Duke loved her intensely, but he was incapable of penetrating her moods. Although their marriage was unhappy, Caroline was not inconsiderate of her husband. However, they moved in different worlds. The Grand Duke would have made an ideal husband for someone, but not for her. Caroline would have made an ideal wife for someone, but not for him. They were not made for each other."[33]

Caroline was often alone as the Grand Duke went out hunting. She barely ate, choosing to nibble on chocolates, almonds and petit fours when she did. She had also taken up smoking.[34] Caroline died on 17 January 1905, just 20 years old. The cause of death was influenza. Hermine wrote, "The attack was so violent that there was no hope of her recovery from the first. She received the tenderest care, but all effort was in vain. In her heart of hearts, she did not wish to live."[35] Caroline's emaciated body simply could not fight the disease. Hermine arrived just two days before her death and found her still conscious but resigned to her fate. The Grand Duke sat by her bed, begging her forgiveness. He promised her that he would change and worship her.[36] Hermine told her sister, "You will be healthy again, you will get out of Weimar, to Emma to Tirol in the Puster Valley. You will get a divorce." To which Caroline replied, "I do not have the strength, let me die..."[37] Hermine described the end as peaceful, the light simply went out.

Without Caroline, Hermine was truly orphaned. "The catastrophe happened so fast that he (Caroline's husband) could not understand. Broken, he sought our comfort, which we gave him. All of Germany mourned with him."[38] The Grand Duchess of Baden (born Luise of Prussia) held Hermine as she sobbed by her sister's deathbed. The Grand Duchess invited Hermine to Karlsruhe and thus became somewhat of a foster-mother to her. The funeral took place on 21 January 1905 and over 20,000 people travelled to Weimar to attend. She was interred in the Fürstengruft in Weimar in a simple sarcophagus. Hermine wrote, "A stranger reigned in place of my father, my mother was dead. My unhappy brother was a burden, no comfort. He found himself unable to cope with life. It is sometimes hard to understand the justice of heaven. Caroline was dead and my brother was alive. When Grand Duchess Luise found me sobbing at my sister's deathbed, she tenderly took me in her arms. And so, the death of my sister gave me a foster mother."[39]

Luise told her, "Come with us to Karlsruhe, you are for me the sacred legacy of our dear dead."[40]

Hermine found a new home in Karlsruhe. She was welcomed warmly by the family and she remained close friends with their daughter Princess Viktoria, who later married the Crown Prince of Sweden. Even after she became Queen of Sweden, Hermine met her every winter in Karlsruhe. In Karlsruhe, Hermine finally found some intellectual stimulation. There were often lectures being held by the professors of the University of

Heidelberg and Hermine often attended them with the Grand Duchess.[41] The Grand Duchess was in regular contact with her niece by marriage, Auguste Viktoria of Schleswig-Holstein, the first wife of the German Emperor. Every week a letter would arrive, and Hermine was tasked with reading the letter to the Grand Duchess, as she suffered from failing eyesight. Hermine described it as, "a strange play of fate."[42] It was her first look into the Imperial court in Berlin. Hermine often joined the Grand Duchess in visiting the studios of the painters of Karlsruhe, such as Schönleber and Volkmann.[43]

Then suddenly rumours appeared that Hermine was to marry her sister's widower. On 22 June 1906, he was on his way to Bückeburg and reportedly, so was Hermine. By mid-July 1906, newspapers announced that an engagement was imminent but the court at Weimar denied this immediately. The engagement did take place, though the Grand Duke had his doubts. Then the engagement was broken off, with no regret on either side.

Chapter 2

First marriage to Prince Johann Georg of Schönaich-Carolath

Hermine wrote very little of the impression she had upon meeting her future first husband, Prince Johann Georg of Schönaich-Carolath. She met him while she was on vacation with relatives in the late summer of 1906. The widowed Princess Marie Alexandrine of Saxe-Weimar-Eisenach was the daughter of Charles Alexander, Grand Duke of Saxe-Weimar-Eisenach and Princess Sophie of the Netherlands, and the wife of the late Prince Heinrich VII Reuss of Köstritz and she took Hermine under her wing after the broken engagement. Princess Marie Alexandrine lived in Trebschen, which was conveniently close to Schloss Saabor where Prince Johann Georg lived. She met Prince Johann Georg and got to know him better. They settled quite quickly on a shared future. Their engagement was announced in the second half of November.

Prince Johann Georg, a lieutenant colonel in the Second Regiment of the Dragoons in Berlin, asked for her hand in marriage at Bückeburg, and her uncle and guardian gave his consent for the marriage on 11 December 1906. On New Year's Eve 1906, the bride and groom appeared together in the registrar's office to make the necessary arrangements for the wedding. Court Marshall Titz von Titzenhofer was tasked with the wedding preparations. The festivities began on 5 January 1907 in Greiz with a "thée dansant", a dance held in the early evening. Hermine wore a light blue crepe dress with silver baubles and lace and carried a bouquet of long-stemmed red roses. January 7th was the actual day of the wedding. At 11 o'clock the civil wedding ceremony took place in the Red Salon. Hermine wore a champagne coloured dress with a blue blouse. At the religious ceremony at 3 o'clock in the afternoon, she wore a white dress of crêpe de chine and a long veil, which had previously been worn by her mother. As the bride and groom exchanged rings, three times 12 cannon shots were fired from the Reissberg.[1]

They honeymooned in Italy, but their social life was off to a bad start when Prince Johann Georg's grandmother died, and the couple was forced into mourning. They would spend the winters in an apartment in Berlin, while they spent the summers in Silesia at Castle Saabor with her parents-in-law.

She received a cordial reception in Saabor by her parents-in-law and became especially close to her father-in-law, who was more like a father to her. He had musical talents and composed small pieces and played the piano. Her mother-in-law, Princess Wanda of Schönaich-Carolath, had been a lady-in-waiting to Empress Auguste. Hermine gave birth to her first child, a son named Hans Georg at the end of 1907. By early 1908, Hermine was back in court life and she and Prince Johann Georg had been invited to luncheon with the Emperor and Empress. It was to be her first meeting with the Emperor since her sister's wedding. She was meeting the Empress for the very first time. At the luncheon she sat to the right of the Emperor and chatted away. He was most interested in her honeymoon to Italy. The conversation led to talk of the occult and one of those present mentioned the reading of tea leaves. As a joke, they all looked at their tea leaves and predicted the future in the silliest way possible.[2] She was shocked to find her husband, who had just been talking with the Empress, suddenly turning very pale. As soon as etiquette allowed them, they hurried home. He assured her that it was nothing, "only a passing spell."[3] But the next morning, he looked like a dying man. He returned from his regiment early and tried to make it up the stairs. He made it but collapsed in a pool of blood that came from his lungs. Hermine described it as consumption in her memoirs, it is now more commonly known as tuberculosis.

Although the marriage was happy and Hermine gave birth to four more children, sons Georg Wilhelm and Ferdinand Johann and daughters Hermine Caroline and Henriette, the story of her first marriage became all about her husband's long illness. "We were always together, in the garden or the fields. We roamed the woods and collected berries and mushrooms and the little ones joined us on our travels to Italian spas where my husband hoped to heal his afflicted lungs."[4] Hermine began to divide her time between Saabor and Italy, where Prince Johann Georg attempted to regain his health. The children went with them to Italy whenever it was possible and according to Hermine, they "proved to be exemplary little travellers."[5] Hermine was entirely responsible for the education of their children. She wrote, "I was their first teacher. My methods were modern. I imparted knowledge playfully in the form of a game, replying truthfully to all questions. My answers were framed in such a way as to be adapted to the age of the child. But it was never necessary for me to correct myself afterward. I never wittingly told an untruth. I avoided even innocent fibs. As a result, the children came to me with all their questions. Until modern psychology began to prod the subconscious, the world never knew how many psychic maladies in adult life may be traced to chance information shockingly imparted to children by strangers. The mental and physical health of children is more important than the transmission of fairy tales designed to guard grown-ups from embarrassing questions. It is not difficult to reveal the mysteries of life to children in terms of plants and flowers. No stork, no Easter rabbit, carrying babies, stalked or leaped through the lives of my children. Their young faith was never shattered by the heart rendering discovery that their mother had lied to them."[6]

Prince Johann Georg invited his regimental comrades to stay for one week every year during which time he tried to conceal his illness. When his comrades had left, he would often be even more ill. The young Hermine was forced into a life of retirement.

They went to Berlin just once or twice a year, where Hermine enjoyed dancing at the Imperial palace. During one of these occasions, she chaperoned Princess Adelheid of Saxe-Meiningen, who would later marry Prince Adalbert of Prussia, the son of the Emperor, and was thus Hermine's future step-daughter-in-law.[7]

Prince Johann Georg was ill for 12 years of their 13-year-long marriage and during this time, the world had begun to change. In 1914, Archduke Franz Ferdinand and his wife Sophie were assassinated in Sarajevo, which kickstarted the First World War. Hermine followed her husband from sanatorium to sanatorium and he was often confined to a wheelchair. Shortly before the outbreak of the First World War, he felt a little better. They returned to Berlin where her husband wished to fight for his country with his beloved regiment. However, the medical staff denied his application. Prince Johann Georg was determined to go and found a place serving with the military under General von Wrochem until he suffered yet another bloody haemorrhage and two attacks of dysentery. He returned to Silesia after this but was assigned to the general command at Breslau until 1917. Hermine often visited him there with the children and in 1917, they took a small apartment in Breslau so that Prince Johann Georg would be more comfortable. In 1914, Prince Johann Georg's only brother was killed during patrol duty.

The war was not only hard on Prince Johann Georg, Hermine too began to suffer from its effects. Fats, meats and bread were sold only with food cards and although Hermine hardly ever stood in line for them – she had maids for that – she began to suffer from a serious gastric disorder that plagued her until long after the war was over.[8] Even the waters at Karlsbad did not cure it.

Towards the end of the First World War, Prince Johann Georg had been appointed economic controller of the German Army of Occupation in Romania. This meant that he was often in Berlin, where Hermine would join him on many occasions.

She wrote, "I was horrified by the naked misery on all sides. Malformed babies with heads too large for their bodies! Weary-eyed children of sixteen that looked like twelve."[9] For three-quarters of the year, Hermine managed a hospital in Saabor, but it was forced to close due to lack of food. Her experiences there had traumatised her. She wrote, "Time cannot wipe out from my memory the tragic and pitiful recollections. Shattered minds, faces no longer recognisable, limbs twisted into fantastic shapes, tortured bodies, groaning with intolerable anguish, conscious of nothing human save pain! All these things I saw. I was one in a multitude of women vainly trying to heal the wounds, to stem the blood of the Fatherland. In every country there were women like myself who beheld the misery rather than the glories of war."[10]

The First World War came to an end in 1918 and in the Imperial Chancellery, Prince Max of Baden, also the last Imperial Chancellor, announced, "His Majesty the Emperor and King has abdicated."[11] Prince Johann Georg returned from Romania, heartbroken and even more ill. Hermine believed that the end of the Empire had given him the final blow to his health. During these dreadful days, Hermine gave birth to her last child, a daughter named Henriette but by the time she was old enough to recognise her father, he was no longer able to hold her. Hermine's homeland too would suffer. The regent of Reuss-Greiz, who ruled in place of Hermine's mentally disabled brother, surrendered the crown.

Eventually, doctors told Hermine that her husband's recovery was out of the question. Hermine devoted her life to his care, together with two nurses. Hermine and Prince Johann Georg travelled to the Black Forest to visit a sanatorium while their children remained behind with their paternal grandmother in Saabor. For the last eight months of his life, Prince Johann Georg was confined to his bed. The children briefly came to see him in August 1919, but they were only allowed to see him from afar.

Prince Johann Georg died on 6 April 1920 in the Wölfelsgrund sanitorium in the Jizera mountains; he was still only 46 years old.[12]

Hermine had to take control back after an absence of a year from her children. She quickly selected schools for the boys, and she took on the management of Saabor, which she found a heavy burden to bear. But after everything, Hermine wrote in her memoirs, "I, thank God, was lucky in my first and in my second marriage."[13] She also wrote, "My chains were pleasant, because they were wrought with the hands of love; nevertheless, they restricted my developed and my freedom. My five children and the Saabor estate were a responsibility. I was handicapped by post-war conditions. The inflation, which destroyed perhaps more wealth than the war, made heavy inroads upon my exchequer. But, at last, I was my own master. I was able to indulge freely in my passion for travel. I travelled, visited towns, exhibitions, theatres, concerts. I renewed my acquaintance with artists and poets. My new freedom enabled me to complete my education and to permit free play to my own personality. I was strongly determined never to marry again, never to surrender the precious right to be the master of my soul."[14]

Chapter 3

The Emperor and Auguste Viktoria

The future Emperor Wilhelm II of Germany was born on 27 January 1859 at 2.45 a.m. as the son of Prince Friedrich of Prussia and Victoria, Princess Royal, the eldest daughter of Queen Victoria of the United Kingdom. Queen Victoria had sent her midwife, Mrs Innocent, and her physician, Sir James Clark. It was a protracted labour, leaving the young Princess in agony. Two professors, Johan Lucas Schoenlein and Eduard Martin, were also in attendance. The baby was in a breech position and Victoria was given chloroform and ergot – a uterine stimulant. He was not breathing when he was born and his left arm was slack.[1] Queen Victoria wrote to her daughter, "God be praised for all his mercies, and for bringing you safely through this awful time! Our joy, our gratitude knows no bounds."[2] He was christened Friedrich Wilhelm Victor Albert on 4 March and the following day Queen Victoria wrote, "Though we cannot be present at this most interesting ceremony, we shall please God! often see our dear grandchild. Poor Grandmama fears she shall never see it, which I told her is nonsense, as please God hereafter it will often come here."[3]

His slack left arm was a cause for great concern and Wilhelm underwent many excruciating treatments to try and fix the problem, like rubbing, binding, surgery and electric shocks. It would always remain shorter than the other arm and Wilhelm went to great lengths to hide it. In exile, he later recalled, "Medical science had not yet adopted modern orthopaedic methods which would be used to treat such a condition today. Whatever the case I was treated in various ways which could only be castigated as unprofessional in the modern world. The only result was that I was in a painful way, greatly tortured."[4] The relationship with his mother was strained from the beginning. She was ashamed that she had given birth to a deformed child but her relationship with Wilhelm's siblings was equally strained. He was joined by seven siblings; Charlotte (born in 1860), Heinrich (born in 1862), Sigismund (born 1864), Viktoria (born 1866), Waldemar (born 1868), Sophia (born 1870) and Margarethe (born 1872). Sigismund tragically died at the age of 22 months of meningitis, followed by Waldemar at the age of 11 of diphtheria.

Until the age of seven, Wilhelm's education was in the hands of women. He received his first lessons from his governess, Sophie von Dobeneck. In 1866, he was allotted a military governor named Captain von Schrötter and a Sergeant Klee was hired to teach him drumming. Barely a year later, von Schrötter was replaced by a first lieutenant named August O'Danne who was later accused of having sex with young boys. His tutor was Georg Hinzpeter who was also appointed in 1866. It was a tough regime for a young boy – but he was a future king in the making. He enjoyed living in Potsdam the most, but the family only lived there in the spring and summer.

On his 10th birthday, Wilhelm was commissioned in the army and he found his new love. In early May, he attended his first military parade. He proudly wrote to his grandmother Queen Victoria, "I marched before the King; he told me that I marched well, but mama said I did it badly."[5] That following spring, he would meet his future wife for the first time when he stayed at Reinhardsbrunn with his parents. Auguste Viktoria of Schleswig-Holstein-Sonderburg-Augustenburg was born on 22 October 1857 as the daughter of Friedrich VIII, Duke of Schleswig-Holstein and Princess Adelheid of Hohenlohe-Langenburg. She would be known in the family as Dona.

In 1871, the Imperial title was revived and now Wilhelm could look to become Emperor as well. Years later Wilhelm wrote, "At last there was to be a German Emperor again. The German Empire had arisen rejuvenated from dust and ashes.

Barbarossa woke from his long sleep. The Ravens of Ryffhäauser disappeared, and the Treasure of the Nibelungs, the Imperial German Crown, rose again out of the green waters of Father Rhine, into the light of the sun, newly-forged by German hands in the fire of battle, studded with the rubies of German blood and with the diamonds of German loyalty! The Prussian eagle and the old German eagle wheeled their flight together in the pure blue of God's heaven!"[6] Wilhelm celebrated his 13th birthday shortly after the Empire was created. His grandfather and namesake had become Emperor Wilhelm I.

On 1 September 1874, Wilhelm was confirmed in the Friedenskirche in Potsdam and Queen Victoria sent the Prince of Wales to represent her. The Prince of Wales later wrote, "Willy went through his examination admirably, and the questions he had to answer must have lasted half an hour. It was a great ordeal for him to go through before the Emperor and Empress and all his family."[7] Later that year, he was sent to a grammar school in Kassel, where the other boys were permitted to omit the "Your Royal Highness" and use the less formal "Sie" or "Prince Wilhelm."[8] He took his final examination in 1877 and passed it, which allowed him to continue his studies at a university. Just before his 18th birthday, he left school. A couple of days later, he was declared to be of age and Queen Victoria gave him the Order of the Bath as a birthday present. He had wanted the Order of the Garter and after making a scene, Queen Victoria granted his wish. It was decided that he should continue his studies at Bonn University. In the six-month interval, he went off to the army.[9]

At Bonn University, he had his own small household and he lived in Villa Frank. He took up classes in law, economics, history, politics, German literature, chemistry, physics and art history. He often spent his weekends visiting family and he also spent much time away from school to attend to royal duties. Auguste Viktoria and Wilhelm only got to know each other better in 1878 when Wilhelm still had his eye on Elisabeth of

Hesse and by Rhine.[10] On 30 August Auguste Viktoria, her sister Karoline Mathilde and their parents visited Potsdam. Wilhelm's father would note in his diary, "Viktoria seems to make quite an impression on Wilhelm."[11] Wilhelm proposed to Auguste Viktoria in April 1879 and he later wrote to her father that his daughter, "has delighted me and carried me away with her whole being and her nature that I immediately resolved with clarity and firmness to devote all my efforts to fighting for her hand."[12] The engagement was announced in June 1880, just six months after Auguste Viktoria's father had passed away suddenly at the age of 50. Queen Victoria approved of the engagement, but Wilhelm's mother had reservations because of his age.[13]

On 27 February 1881, Wilhelm and Auguste Viktoria were married in Berlin. Among the royal guests were the Prince of Wales, Alfred, Duke of Edinburgh and King Albert and Queen Carola of Saxony. Auguste Viktoria had six bridesmaids who were in charge of carrying her long train. Wilhelm recorded in his diary, "I was married to-day in the chapel of the Castle. We shall settle in Potsdam, where I am to continue my service in the Hussars of the Guards."[14] Just two months after their own wedding, they attended the wedding of Crown Prince Rudolf of Austria and Princess Stéphanie of Belgium. By the autumn it became clear that Auguste Viktoria was expecting their first child and a son was born to them at the Marble Palace on 6 May 1882. He was a little more elaborate in his diary that day. "My son was born to-day. He is the first heir to the German Empire, and I feel that I have performed my duty towards this Empire, in providing our dynasty with a successor in the direct line. My grandfather is so happy, far happier than my father, at least outwardly. He never expected to have his wish granted before he died, to see his family continued by me. In the country, also, the event has been hailed with immense joy, and I have received any amount of congratulations."[15] Wilhelm's mother was annoyed that the new Prince was named Wilhelm and not Friedrich for his grandfather.[16]

It soon became clear that Wilhelm and Auguste Viktoria had very little in common. Daisy, Princess of Pless wrote, "For a woman in that position, I have never met anyone so devoid of any individual thought or agility of brain and understanding. She is just like a good, quiet soft cow that has calves and eats grass slowly and then lies down and ruminates."[17] The young Auguste Viktoria was in awe of Wilhelm's so-called cleverness and was brought up to believe that she needed to give her husband sons. And that she did. Eitel Friedrich was born in 1883, Adalbert in 1884, August Wilhelm in 1887, Oskar in 1888, Joachim in 1890 and finally a daughter named Viktoria Luise in 1892. While Wilhelm was still second in line to the throne, the couple saw very little of each other. They had breakfast together before Wilhelm headed off to his military duties. He would often return to the Palace for lunch and if there were no further commitments in the afternoon, they would sometimes go for a ride together.

By 1887, it became clear that Wilhelm's father the Crown Prince was ill and that he might become Emperor sooner than expected. The first signs of throat cancer appeared in January 1887 and his hoarse voice became a cause for concern. Symptoms persisted and one of the doctors thought he noticed signs of cancer and tried to remove the lump with a wire loop. It ended up becoming a medical quarrel between doctors. For now, the public only knew that the Crown Prince was suffering from a severe cold.[18] Friedrich had several growths removed and he travelled to take the waters – nothing was helping. When Wilhelm suggested an operation that might help his father, his mother accused him of wanting to accelerate his father's death. "She treated me like a dog. She feared above all the collapse of the house of cards upon which she had based her hopes... Standing at the bottom of the stairs, I was obliged to hear her reproaches at my behaviour and accept her decisive refusal to let me see my father; I was to leave immediately and continue my journey on to Rome." His father then came out of his room and greeted his son with a smile and "in the following difficult days we both came inwardly very close to one another."[19]

Emperor Wilhelm I passed away on 9 March 1888 and Wilhelm's father succeeded as Emperor Friedrich III. It was to be a short reign as the new Emperor was already dying of throat cancer. He was unable to speak for all of the 99 days of his reign. On 15 June 1888, Wilhelm's father passed away and Wilhelm ascended the throne as the third Emperor of the year. Queen Victoria wrote to her granddaughter Princess Viktoria of Hesse and by Rhine, "It is too dreadful for us all to think of Willy & Bismarck & Dona – being the supreme head of all now! Two so unfit & one so wicked."[20] Queen Victoria wrote to her newly widowed daughter, "Darling, darling, unhappy Child, I clasp you in my arms and to a heart that bleeds, for this is a double, dreadful grief, a misfortune untold and to the world at large. You are far more sorely tried than me. I had not the agony of seeing another fill the place of my angel husband which I always felt I never could have borne. May God help and support you as He did me and may your children be some help, some comfort, as so many of mine were. Though at that time there was bitterness. I can't write what I feel. I can't collect my thoughts. I feel stunned. I would wish to do anything and everything to help you, even to go to you if you wished. Do come to us. You should get quite away with the girls for a time. Your health will require it after such a long strain. Darling beloved Fritz, I loved him so dearly. He was so kind to me always and in '61. I see him always before me with those beautiful, loving blue eyes. How well he was here last year still. Here you were engaged and here I received the dreadful news. I am so thankful other people have aggravated all were not there... God in His mercy help and support you."[21]

Wilhelm considered the monarch to be the symbol of the empire "whose progresses were there to encourage the people through a constantly renewed pageant."[22] Wilhelm travelled as much as he could, and he was only in Berlin and Potsdam half of the year. Later in the early days of his exile he told a staff officer, "My grandfather felt himself above all to be the King of Prussia. Being Emperor meant more to him as a title than for its content. I had no historical precedents to fall back on and was born to the position of German Emperor. I had to spin new threads between the headship of the Empire and the German people, in order to be true to my God-given German mission; I had to bring together all its diverse strengths and produce in every German a proud consciousness of *civis germanus*."[23]

By 1897, Auguste Viktoria had given birth to seven children and she had had at least one or two miscarriages. She was also suffering from a nervous condition for some years, which became worse. At the end of 1897, she had suffered a "severe nervous shock" and did not recover until the following April. She was under constant physical strain to keep her figure since Wilhelm did not like plump women. He also ensured that she had a regular supply of diet pills.[24]

In early 1901 just as Prussia was celebrating the bicentenary of the Hohenzollern dynasty it became clear that Wilhelm's grandmother Queen Victoria was dying. The remaining celebrations were promptly cancelled, and Wilhelm travelled to Osborne to join the rest of the family. Wilhelm wrote to the British Ambassador in Berlin, "I have duly informed the Prince of Wales, begging him that no notice whatever is taken of me as Emperor and that I come as a grandson. I suppose the "petticoats" who are fencing off poor grandmamma from the world – and I fear, often from me – will kick up a row when they hear of my coming; but I don't care for what I do is my duty, the more so as it is this "unparalleled" grandmamma, as none ever existed before. I leave with Uncle Arthur. Am sorry, very sorry."[25] Queen Victoria died on 22 January 1901 with Wilhelm by her side.

Meanwhile, Auguste Viktoria travelled to Friedrichshof to be with Wilhelm's mother, Empress Friedrich, who was also slowly dying of cancer. Both Auguste Viktoria and Wilhelm were by her side when the Empress passed away on 5 August 1901. The Emperor immediately sent his officers to ransack all of his mother's desks to seize any private letters, but most had already been sent to England for safekeeping. He later told the Tsar of Russia, "The suffering was so terrible that one could look upon the end as a release."[26] Around this time, Auguste Viktoria discovered she was pregnant again at the age of 42. She went to great efforts to hide the pregnancy from her husband and defied her doctor's orders when he told her to rest. The following month, she suffered a miscarriage.

The deaths of both Queen Victoria and the Empress Friedrich only reinforced Auguste Viktoria's antipathy towards all things English. In November 1902, her husband was invited to Sandringham for King Edward VII's birthday, but Auguste Viktoria did not accompany him. Her son said, "My mother is always in a fever if I or my father go to England."[27] She would be fond of her daughter-in-law Cecilie of Mecklenburg-Schwerin who married her eldest son the Crown Prince on 6 June 1905. It was Auguste Viktoria who placed the Prussian bridal crown on Cecilie's head just before the ceremony and afterwards she told her son what a good choice he had made. In turn, Cecilie became very fond of her mother-in-law.[28] With six sons, more daughters-in-law soon followed. Their second son, Prince Eitel Friedrich, met Sophie Charlotte of Oldenburg at his brother's wedding and their engagement was announced in October 1905. They married in February 1906, but it was by no means a happy love match. He continued his affairs while Sophie Charlotte remained at her castle in Tiergarten to paint. Their first grandchild was born on 4 July 1906 and he was duly named Wilhelm. Auguste Viktoria was there to support Cecilie as the Crown Prince quickly resumed the hunting trip he had interrupted when he heard that Cecilie had gone into labour.[29]

In late 1907, Auguste Viktoria could no longer avoid everything English. In November, she and her husband paid a state visit to the United Kingdom. Her plan to claim she had to nurse her daughter through the chickenpox fell through when Viktoria Luise improved. Several other foreign royals were also at Windsor, but Auguste Viktoria apparently made no effort to be friendly with them. After the state visit, the Emperor went to Highcliffe Castle, while Auguste Viktoria went to the Netherlands to meet Queen Wilhelmina.[30] On 22 October 1908, their fourth son August Wilhelm married his first cousin Alexandra Viktoria of Schleswig-Holstein-Sonderburg-Glücksburg. It was also Auguste Viktoria's 50th birthday. Yet again, this would prove to be an unhappy marriage.[31]

The fourth of their children to marry was their only daughter Viktoria Luise. Her future husband was Prince Ernst August of Hanover who had come to Berlin to meet the Emperor and to thank him. His elder brother Georg had been killed in a car crash on his way to Denmark for the funeral of their uncle King Frederick VIII of Denmark. His car had skidded off the road near Nackel in Brandenburg and the Emperor had insisted that the Crown Prince and Prince Eitel Friedrich should form part of the guard of honour that would escort the body to its final resting place.

Viktoria Luise was smitten with Prince Ernst August and the wedding was set for 24 May 1913. It was to be the last great gathering of foreign royals before the outbreak of the First World War. Among the guests were King George V and Queen Mary, Tsar Nicholas II of Russia (not accompanied by his wife), and the Dowager Duchess of Baden, Luise. Auguste Viktoria took her daughter's departure very hard and the following day she invited Viktoria Luise's former governess for dinner.[32]

In June 1913, the silver jubilee of Wilhelm's accession to the throne was celebrated. The celebrations were all too much for

Auguste Viktoria and at the banquet she collapsed and had to be taken to her rooms. She had not been in the best of health for a while now. The situation was probably not helped when her fifth son, Prince Oskar fell in love with Countess Ina von Bassewitz-Levetzow who had been appointed one of the Empress's ladies-in-waiting. Their relationship had been a secret at first but a probably drunken Prince Eitel Friedrich attacked Ina one night. Prince Oskar heard her screaming, ran to her and knocked his brother to the ground. He then declared to his mother that he loved Ina and intended to marry her. If they were forbidden to marry, he was prepared to go into exile and marry her anyway. Augusta Viktoria realised there was little chance of Oskar ever succeeding to the throne and asked her husband for his permission. His first reaction was anger. He ordered Ina to leave Berlin and never to return. Ina obeyed with the hope that he would eventually relent. For several weeks, Prince Oskar and his mother pleaded with the Emperor and even received the support of Viktoria Luise. Viktoria Luise had just given birth to a son and when he was about to be christened, her father asked what she would like as a present. Viktoria Luise told him that she really wanted permission for her brother to be allowed to marry the love of his life. The Emperor eventually conceded and the engagement between Prince Oskar and Ina was announced on 26 May 1914.[33] Just a month later, all hell broke loose.

On 28 June 1914, Archduke Franz Ferdinand of Austria, heir to the throne, and his morganatic wife Sophie were assassinated during a visit to Sarajevo. The following month, the German ambassador was informed that total Russian mobilisation had taken place and the Emperor too ordered a full mobilisation of the German troops. Prince Oskar was about to take up command and quickly arranged for Ina to come to Berlin for a small private wedding. On 31 July 1914, they married at the Bellevue Palace with the Emperor and Empress present. Ina was not created a Princess but was instead given the title of Countess von

Ruppin. That same day, Wilhelm wired his cousins, the Tsar of Russia and the King of the United Kingdom, "It is not I who bears the responsibility for the disaster which now threatens the entire civilised world. Even at this moment the decision to stave it off with lies with you. No one threatens the honour or power of Russia. The friendship for you and your empire which I have borne from the deathbed of my grandfather has always been totally sacred to me... the peace of Europe can still be maintained by you, if Russia decided to halt the military measures which threaten Germany and Austria-Hungary. For technical reasons the mobilisation I ordered this afternoon had to be effected on the eastern and western front. The order sadly cannot be countermanded because your telegram arrived so late. However, were France to offer me her neutrality, which must be guaranteed by the British army and navy, I will naturally refrain from attacking France and employ my troops elsewhere. I hope that France will not be nervous. The troops on my borders will be immediately telephonically and telegraphically stopped me from crossing the French frontier. Wilhelm."[34]

On 1 August 1914, Germany declared war on Russia. Two days later, Germany declared war on France. Right in the middle of all this, another wedding took place. On 3 August 1914, their third son Prince Adalbert married his second cousin Princess Adelheid of Saxe-Meiningen, whom he had been courting for several years. They had a simple military wedding in the chapel of the naval base where Prince Adalbert was stationed with the SMS Prinzregent Luitpold. On 4 August, the United Kingdom declared war on Germany. The Emperor left for the front on 12 August 1914 and Auguste Viktoria wrote him a letter of assurance. "But God will bring you back to me in good health, that is what you must always tell yourself whenever your poor nerves and your poor heart feel so depressed. Then you must always remember that I sense it from afar, (and) even though I cannot be with you, in my prayers I am always close to you and will try to calm you. Don't take it all so much to heart, my darling, you can face the world with a clear conscience. Your country is fighting calmly for its holiest values and the Lord will show it the war forward."[35] Auguste Viktoria threw herself into the war effort. She went around visiting hospitals and appealed to the women of Germany to do their part. Food rationing and fuel shortages meant that petitions to the Empress increased. She moved from the Stadtschloss to the Bellevue Palace to save money and set an example. Meanwhile, she was keeping an eye on her ever-growing family. Adalbert's wife Adelheid gave birth to a sickly daughter named Viktoria Marina on 4 September 1915, who tragically only lived for a few hours. Auguste Viktoria was grieved at the loss of her grandchild and began to have troubles with her heart and back. She also began to suffer from depression. There was nothing more she could for her husband, who alternated between utter despair and dreams of victory.[36] Meanwhile, she was also busy arranging a marriage between their youngest son Prince Joachim and Princess Marie Auguste of Anhalt. However, he had embroiled himself in a scandal involving the jewellery of his equerry's sister and Auguste Viktoria was deeply upset. He had asked to use the jewellery to pledge them temporarily to settle some debts but once he had them, he had sold them. Prince Joachim feared his father's reaction and immediately went to Princess Marie Auguste to propose to perhaps lessen the blow. On 11 March 1916, they married at the Bellevue Palace with only a few guests. The Emperor did not return from Spa for the wedding and both Auguste Viktoria and Joachim were hurt by his absence.[37]

Auguste Viktoria began to frequently visit her husband while he was at his headquarters and took it upon herself to act as an intermediary between the Emperor, General Hindenburg, Admiral Tirpitz, General Gröner and others. Her popularity soared as she was seen as the one most concerned for the general welfare of the German people. In July 1918, as the Emperor was beginning to lose his resolve, Auguste Viktoria visited the headquarters at Spa to support him. She encouraged him to be an autocrat and not to accept any demands from the government or from Prince Max of Baden, who would become the last chancellor.[38]

It all became too much for her and in August 1918 she suffered a stroke that left her partially paralysed. She was ordered to complete rest and she was confined to her bed. Shortly after, the Emperor too had some sort of breakdown and when she heard of this, she pulled herself from her bed to spent time with him to restore his confidence. When the news came that Tsar Nicholas II and his family had been massacred in a basement in Ekaterinburg, she was horrified, despite her long antipathy towards his wife. Wilhelm left Potsdam for Spa on 29 October and he collapsed into tears when saying goodbye to his wife. It was to be the last time she would see him as Emperor.[39]

That very day, sailors from the Imperial navy mutinied and took the ports of Kiel and Wilhelmshaven. Revolutionaries took over the cities of Hanover, Frankfurt and Munich and railway lines were cut to prevent the sending of reinforcements. From Spa, Wilhelm wrote his wife several letters, but they did not arrive as the postal stations were in the hands of the revolutionaries. On 9 November, Prince Max of Baden, now Chancellor, was told by the Allied forces that the Emperor would need to renounce the throne to ensure peace. With reluctance, Wilhelm declared he would be willing to step down as German Emperor but that he would remain as King of Prussia. Auguste Viktoria was at the Neues Palais in Potsdam, waiting for news. Even as hostile troops approached, Auguste Viktoria refused to leave.[40]

In retrospect, Wilhelm believed he had done the right thing. "If I had stayed, the German people might have been forced to shameful compliance with the Allied demand for my surrender. I am responsible to God; I am responsible for my country; but I am not, and was not, responsible to my people's foes. I had to choose between sacrificing myself and sacrificing my country. I sacrificed myself. It is not my fault that the sacrifice was in vain."[41]

On 10 November 1918, Wilhelm crossed the border into the Netherlands and requested asylum at the train station at Eijsden at six in the morning. A Dutch sergeant and his men refused to allow the Emperor entrance into the Netherlands because they had had no orders to allow him in. As the news reached The Hague, Wilhelm spent several anxious hours at the Eijsden train station. He was finally granted political asylum and was to be received by the Count of Aldenburg-Bentinck at Amerongen Castle. The Count's son was serving as an officer in the German navy. Queen Wilhelmina of the Netherlands was awoken very early that morning to receive the news that the German Emperor was at the border. She later wrote in her memoirs, "I am not overreacting when I say that it had taken me a week or maybe even longer before I could believe the incoming messages, that is how improbable this action seemed to me."[42]

For Queen Wilhelmina, the Emperor's flight went against everything she believed in as a sovereign. There was also the rumour that Wilhelm had come invited as one of Queen Wilhelmina's adjutants, former Governor-General Van Heutsz, who was pro-German, had visited the German headquarters at Spa shortly before the Emperor fled to the Netherlands. However, this visit had been planned long in advance and no invitation was issued to Wilhelm. He had also had lunch with Wilhelm on 8 November. An invitation from Queen Wilhelmina was also, considering her own convictions, rather improbable. She never visited the Emperor in Amerongen or in Doorn. If anything needed to be discussed, she used the Count van Lynden van Sandenburg as a liaison. However, the possibility of an arrangement cannot be dismissed outright. Queen Wilhelmina intentionally destroyed several items in the archives from around this time and the speed with which the decision was made to allow Wilhelm entry into the country makes one wonder.[43] Wilhelm and Auguste Viktoria were quite saddened by Queen Wilhelmina's lack of interest in them. Even Crown Princess Cecilie, a niece of Queen Wilhelmina's husband Hendrik, did not receive an answer to a letter she had sent.[44] Wilhelm re-boarded the Imperial train, and Sigurd von Ilsemann described the following journey. "In all the cities, villages and even along the tracks people lined up in the thousands. All the way to Arnhem there was screaming, whistling, raised fists and people gesturing the cutting off of their head. It was outright repulsive. Why could they not have spared the Emperor this?"[45]

A newspaper reported the Emperor's arrival in Maarn, "Yet, the fallen ruler looks calm, when he leaves his carriage, kindly greeted by his host Baron Bentinck, who introduces him to the provincial governor and the internment-general Onnen. [...] Outside there is some cheering when the ex-Emperor becomes visible and a single hiss sounds through, but the public remains dignified."[46]

A telegram was sent from the station at Eijsden to Queen Wilhelmina. "As a result of the events, I have been forced, as a private person, to enter your country and put myself under the protection of your government. The hope that you have taken account of my difficult situation has not disappointed me, and I sincerely thank you and your Government for the kind hospitality I have received."[47]

Auguste Viktoria believed her place was by her husband's side and the newly formed Council of People's Commissars granted her permission to go to the Netherlands. Her husband had given them his word that he would abdicate. Prince Eitel Friedrich, fearing for his mother's safety, requested that she come stay with him at Villa Ingenheim for the time being and she left just in time. Soon crowds broke in to the Neues Palais and ransacked the ground floor. Even at Villa Ingenheim she was not safe. A group of sailors broke in and interrogated the Empress, who faced them bravely. By the end of the month, she had done most of her packing. On 27 November, she left Potsdam for the last time. Cecilie drove her mother-in-law to the Charlottenburg Station where a specially prepared black train was waiting for her. She sat in the back of the train with Countess Keller.[48]

The following day, she joined her husband at Amerongen in the Netherlands, alighting at Maarsbergen station to avoid a scene.[49] That very same day, her husband formally signed the document of abdication as German Emperor and King of Prussia. The revolutionary government permitted the transfer of one million marks to the Emperor's accounts in the Netherlands.[50] When Auguste Viktoria arrived the castle, he stood alone on the bridge over the moat where he stood to attention and gave her a military salute. She ran over and embraced him. A small suite of rooms had been set aside for her on the upper floor of the castle. She would only allow the Countess Keller into her presence and often ate meals alone. She wrote to her daughter, "Perhaps I would get some strength back if I had something to do in my own home. Here, I always have melancholy thoughts and, at the most, letters to write."[51] Despite her melancholy, the former Emperor and Empress were still living the life of luxury, though perhaps not to the extent they had known before. They had been able to take 25 carts of personal items, a car and a boat. Several properties were theirs personally and this was acknowledged by the government. Large sums were tied up in stocks and they still had servants.[52]

Early in 1919, there were calls on the Dutch government to extradite Wilhelm on charges of war crimes. The indignant Dutch replied that they had a right to offer hospitality to whomsoever they pleased.[53] In any case, the Emperor did not intend to fall into enemy hands. "I do not want to be dragged through the streets of Paris or London like the most evil criminal and to be beheaded by the bastards. Let there be no doubt: If I am in their hands, they will kill me. I cannot do that shame and disgrace to myself, my house or Germany: I won't let my enemies have that triumph."[54] When the matter of extradition was finally settled, the Emperor was relieved. "Thank God, this torture is over, it lasted a year and half. Just imagine Ilsemann, what I have lived through in that time! And then my poor wife; it nearly killed her!"[55]

In August 1919, Wilhelm bought House Doorn, not too far from Amerongen, for half a million guilders.[56] Just before moving out of Amerongen, Elisabeth, daughter of the Count of Aldenburg-Bentinck, wrote of Wilhelm, "He does not have a strong character and is unable to make independent decisions in difficult matters. He is afraid to hear the truth and avoids unpleasant subjects. He does not enjoy working alone or having to entertain himself. If at all possible, he needs to be near someone. He most enjoys talking, talking and talking some more and to let admiring people hear him. He never grows tired, but his audience does."[57]

They moved in the following year. Shortly after Wilhelm bought the house, the Prussian Finance Minister agreed to the transfer of furniture and works of art from the Berlin Schloss, Schloss Bellevue, Schloss Charlottenburg and the Neues Palais in Potsdam. By then, Auguste Viktoria's health was so bad that a lift had to be installed to get her to the top floor. Nevertheless, she enjoyed furnishing their new house. In October, a contract was signed between the Hohenzollerns and the Prussian State by which 20 of the 60 formerly royal castles were deemed to be the family's property. This contract also included a lump sum of 32 million marks and 24,000 Dutch guilders.[58]

Around this time, several of her children's marriages were falling apart. The Crown Prince and Cecilie were living apart. Prince Eitel Friedrich and Sophia Charlotte were both having extra-marital affairs, but they did not divorce until 1926. Prince Joachim and Marie Auguste had one son together in

1916 and were now barely speaking. Prince August Wilhelm and Alexandra Viktoria had one son together as well, but they divorced in March 1920. Prince Adalbert and Adelheid were living in Switzerland with their two children, and Prince Oskar and Ina were happy with their three children, but they were the exceptions. In June 1920, the Emperor bestowed the style and title of Her Royal Highness and Princess of Prussia upon Ina.[59]

On 13 July 1920, Auguste Viktoria suffered a heart attack and was bedridden. Her daughter Viktoria Luise and her husband arrived later in the week. Then on 18 July 1920, Prince Joachim, who had suffered from depression and gambling problems, shot himself. He was found and taken to the hospital, where he died a few hours later. The Emperor decided that Auguste Viktoria must not be told of his suicide, for fear of causing another heart attack. He did tell her that their youngest son had died, but he told her it was an accident. She probably realised the truth and took the news with "the usual composure she exhibited when fate dealt her severe blows." The Emperor and Empress were denied entry into Germany to attend their son's funeral and were only able to send a large wreath. Joachim's son was briefly in the custody of his uncle Prince Eitel Friedrich until the courts decided that he should be returned to his mother. While he was in his uncle's custody, he was often at Doorn and Auguste Viktoria watched him from a wheelchair while he played in the garden.[60]

On 22 October, Auguste Viktoria celebrated her 62nd birthday but she spent the day in bed, hardly able to move. She then suffered several heart attacks and by November she was in and out of consciousness. Yet she rallied but continued to spend her days in bed. When her brother Ernst Gunther died on 22 January 1921, she wasn't informed. Shortly after midnight on 11 April 1921, her breathing suddenly changed and her pulse gradually weakened. She passed away at around 5.30 in the morning.

She had told her daughter, "I will sleep in my homeland" and it was her express wish that she be buried in Potsdam. It was finally agreed that she could be interred in the royal mausoleum at the Neues Palais in Potsdam as long as there was little fanfare nor any official ceremony. The Emperor was not allowed to attend the funeral and could only accompany her coffin to the border. Princes Oskar and Adalbert would accompany their mother, while Princes August Wilhelm and Eitel Friedrich went ahead to make the preparations. On 17 April her coffin was taken to Maarn station where a small memorial service was held. The train left early the following morning, but the Emperor found that he could not return to the station to see it leave. The train passed through several stations, which all had their flags at half-mast, before crossing the border into Germany around 10 in the morning. Around 10,000 people reportedly lined the tracks.[61] The Emperor wrote, "What every common worker can do, namely follow his wife's coffin to the grave, even that has been made impossible for me by my traitorous people!"[62]

Wilhelm would turn his wife's bedroom into a shrine with a cross of flowers across her bed. He would go there at least once a week to mourn his wife.[63] In his memoirs, he wrote of his wife, "The revolution broke the Empress's heart. She aged visibly from November 1918 onward, and could not resist her bodily ills with her previous strength. Thus, her decline soon began. The hardest of all for her to bear was her homesickness for Germany, for the German people. Notwithstanding this, she still tried to afford consolation for me."[64]

With his wife's death, the Emperor's isolation increased. Several women began to flock to House Doorn, hoping to become Germany's new Empress, if only in name. A Finnish female Doctor Hammar, who claimed to be clairvoyant, managed to fascinate Wilhelm with her predications of his restoration and demanded that he marry her on several occasions. Two Hungarian sisters also reportedly left a deep impression. Other women included Princess Luise of Solms, Ittel von Tschirschky, Archduchess Marie Christine of Austria – the widowed Hereditary Princess of

Salm-Salm – Catalina von Pannwitz and Gabriele von Rochow. He had openly discussed the option of remarriage with Cornelia Johanna (Lily) van Heemstra, whose great-aunt had owned House Doorn, and who had already been romantically linked to the Crown Prince. He wrote her a sexually explicit letter, which she then showed to the Crown Prince, in which he asked her to become his concubine. She was later briefly engaged to Prince Wolfgang of Hesse.[65]

The Emperor's eventual choice of Hermine Reuss of Greiz may have been with an eye to a restoration. She was, at least, of royal blood.

Wilhelm with first wife Auguste Viktoria and their children in 1896
Bundesarchiv Bild 146-2008-0152 / Julius Cornelius Schaarwächter

Amerongen Castle – where Wilhelm first arrived in 1918.
Photo by the author

House Doorn
Photo by the author

Saabor Castle circa 1926/1938
Bundesarchiv Bild 102-00954/Georg Pahl

Hermine with her children at Schloss Saabor in Silesia in
November 1927 (L-R Georg Wilhelm, Hans Georg, Hermine,
Henriette, Hermine Caroline and Ferdinand Johann)
Bundesarchiv Bild 102-05029/Georg Pahl

Hermine and Wilhelm in the grounds of House Doorn in
January 1926
Bundesarchiv Bild 102-03452/Unknown

Hermine and Wilhelm with her daughter Henriette "the General" in the grounds of House Doorn in January 1929
Bundesarchiv Bild 102-11383/Unknown

Hermine and Wilhelm at House Doorn in September 1933
Bundesarchiv Bild 136-C0805/Oscar Tellgmann

The Old Palace in Berlin - where Hermine had apartments. It was damaged in 1943 but the façade remained intact.

Photo by the author

Wedding of Hermine Caroline and Hugo Hartung on 10 December 1936

Bundesarchiv Bild 102-17735/Georg Pahl

Wedding of Prince Ludwig Ferdinand of Prussia and Grand
Duchess Kira Kirillovna of Russia on 4 May 1938 at House Doorn –
Photographer unknown/Nationaal Archief/Fotocollectie Elsevier

Wilhelm's funeral on 9 June 1941
Bundesarchiv Bild 101I-224-0008-00/Lassberg

The mausoleum at Doorn where Wilhelm was interred.
Photo by the author

The Antique Temple in Potsdam where both Hermine and Auguste
Viktoria (and four of her sons) are interred.
Photo by the author

Chapter 4

Marriage to the Emperor

Shortly before Easter 1922, a young Prince Georg Wilhelm walked up to his mother at their estate in Saabor as she was handling the bills. In a tearful voice, he told his mother how sorry he felt for the Emperor, who was now all alone. "Mama, when I grow up, I want to fight for the Emperor!" he told her. "Mama, can I write him a letter?" he asked her. And so, he did.

"To His Majesty the Emperor,
Dear Kaiser,
I am only a little boy, but I want to fight for you when I am a man. I am sorry because you are so terribly lonely. Easter is coming. Mama will give us cake and coloured eggs. But I would gladly give up the cakes and the eggs, if only I could bring you back. There are many little boys like me who love you.
Georg Wilhelm, Prince of Schönaich-Carolath"[1]

He had to copy the letter after tears had blotted the paper, but Hermine did not make him alter the letter. It came straight from the heart of a child. The boy addressed the envelope himself and insisted on posting it at once. Surprisingly, the Emperor responded within a few days. "Mama, mama, a letter from the Emperor!" Georg Wilhelm shouted. The envelope contained two letters and a photo of the Emperor. One of the letters was addressed to Georg Wilhelm, but the other was addressed to his mother. It was the first letter she had ever received from the Emperor. The Emperor thanked Hermine for Georg Wilhelm's letter and he included an invitation for Georg Wilhelm and her to visit him at House Doorn. Hermine was speechless.[2]

The Emperor later said of receiving the letter, "Soon after that she (Empress Auguste Viktoria) died. Without her, life was almost too heavy a burden. I would not have been able to carry on if it had not been for my faith in God. My children were far away. They had their own tasks, their own families. I was alone with myself and my sorrow. I prayed to God that He should send some token, some sign of His fatherly love, something to give me new strength to complete my mission. At that moment my eyes fell on a letter on my writing desk. This letter was from a little boy in Silesia, who expressed his sympathy for my loss and my loneliness with the stark simplicity and complete sincerity of a child. For some reason the child's letter touched me deeply. It seemed to me like a sign from heaven. The heart of the child went out to his Emperor in exile and in sorrow. There was no pretence. There was no design. He was completely himself. I looked at the signature and recognised the name – Schönaich-Carolath. I had never met the boy. I casually knew his father, the late Prince Schönaich-Carolath, one of my officers in the Guards. Since that time the avalanche of the World War had descended upon me. I had pleasant but faint impressions of the boy's mother, the Princess Hermine. Several of my gentlemen knew the Princess well and encouraged me to invite her to Doorn. I was so pleased with the lad's letter that I asked his mother to visit me with her children."[3]

Hermine weighed the pros and cons and decided against interrupting the schooling of her sons. She had heard stories of the Emperor's sadness and decided against bringing her daughters, whom she did not want to see affected by any possible sadness. She decided to go alone.[4] On 7 June 1922, Hermine left Saabor by train and headed for Doorn. She was briefly held up in Bad Bentheim, the last German station before the Netherlands. The Dutch conductor noticed the final destination on her ticket and asked if she was going to see the Emperor. She answered yes and he approvingly told her that it was a good thing as the Emperor must be very lonely. The conductor shared an anecdote with her about the Emperor's son, he does not mention which one, also being on this train and helping him with the luggage. The entire journey lasted 18 hours. She disembarked in Amersfoort as Doorn had no railway station.[5] She was met at Amersfoort by General von Dommes, a confidant of the Emperor. He accompanied her by car to Doorn.

The Emperor, dressed in a grey uniform, stood on the steps in front of House Doorn to welcome her where he presented her with a beautiful red rose. The Emperor said of that meeting, "When I saw her, I was immediately profoundly stirred. I was fascinated. I instantly recognised that she was my mate. 'Spring comes but once a year, love but once in a lifetime', the poet sings. But the poet lies. Love may come twice in a lifetime. Blessed indeed is the man to whom love comes a second time. I am not referring to mere trivial affections, but to deep fundamental emotions that shake the very root of our being. I saw in her the messenger of love sent to me by heaven."[6]

For Hermine, it was her first meeting with the Emperor in nine years. They had last talked at Breslau, where she had also met with the late Empress. In her memoirs, she described the Emperor, "The Emperor's hair is snowy white. It was beginning to turn grey when I saw him last. How changed he looks with his beard! The white frame accentuates the spirituality of his features. His carriage is firm and youthful. He does not look like a man who permits fate to bend his back. His Majesty stands before me in a simple field-grey uniform. With native chivalry he helps me out of the car. Gallantly he kisses my hand and conducts me with elastic steps into his home under alien stars. His Majesty insists on taking me to my room."[7]

Quite unusually, Hermine had two rooms in the house itself. These rooms had previously been lived in by the Emperor's younger sister, Princess Margarethe, Landgravine of Hesse and were called "the Hessian apartments." As the house was quite small, visitors to Doorn were often housed in hotels in the area. The Emperor left her and her maid, Frau Sturm, alone to freshen up.[8]

They met again in the dining room where Hermine was surprised at the Emperor's easy-going demeanour. Hermine described how she forgot all about the long journey and how tired she was because of the Emperor's animated conversation. The next morning, Hermine watched from her room as the Emperor walked in the park, as he did every morning. He cut roses for her and handed them to her when she joined him in the park later.[9] In the Auguste Viktoria Rose Garden, the Emperor said, "Never have the roses had this much colour and scent as now. The Empress is dead, but her roses are still alive. She loved them so much. Every bush was precious to her and she could sit in her chair in the cabin and watch her roses for hours."[10] The Emperor showed her around the house, and Hermine noted that she found it small for someone who was used to palaces. They even went into the room where Auguste Viktoria died, which was still left the way it was. Hermine noted that the ghost of the deceased still lived in the room. Even after Hermine moved into Doorn, she would not be allowed to use the room, even though it was one of the best in the house.[11] She wrote in her memoirs, "The room of the departed Empress remains as it was when she died. Not a picture is changed, not a chair is moved. It is the largest and sunniest room in House Doorn. Like the rose garden, named in her honour, it remains dedicated to the memory of Auguste Viktoria. At least once every week the Emperor visits the room where her faithful heart ceased to beat, reverently and alone, to commune with his memories. I conduct the most faithful among those who make a pilgrimage to House Doorn, no less reverently than the Emperor herself, to the shrine of the martyred Empress. Deprived of her crown, Auguste Viktoria still wears a halo. No one can enter the room that had seen so much sorrow and suffering without being visibly moved."[12]

Every day of Hermine's visit, she and the Emperor walked in the park and talked. General von Dommes asked her after a few days, "What have you done to the Emperor?" Hermine was alarmed but the General meant it well. The Emperor had completely changed his routine and had no time to listen to the General's rapports. His secretaries had a few days off as the Emperor had not written a single letter in the days of Hermine's visit. "Since Your Highness has been here, the dark clouds have disappeared from above the Emperor's head. He no longer walks around like a figure from a Greek tragedy. You have made him human again. There is new light in his eyes and in his attitude."[13]

That same afternoon, Hermine and the Emperor had tea in the room of the only tower of the house. Suddenly, he took her hands in his and asked her to become his wife. Hermine described it as being struck by lightning. Hermine had only been a widow for two years; the Emperor had only been widowed for year. She had achieved independence during this time and a freedom that she had never felt before. Marrying the Emperor would mean giving up a lot of that. She remembered the childhood dreams she had had about her dream prince. What were the odds of ending up with your childhood dream? The Emperor seemed to understand the struggle that Hermine was going through, and he gave her time to think.

"Your Majesty, I am afraid I cannot make you happy. I am no one compared to the deceased Empress, I am a completely different kind of woman. I am Hermine, not Auguste Viktoria! Your Majesty would try to find traits in me that endeared you in Empress Auguste Viktoria and you find that I do not possess them. For forty years, the deceased Empress was your daily companion and those forty years cannot be forgotten by any successor. I am independent and I trust myself. After the first romantic emotions, we would probably see that we have made a mistake. Right now the air is full of roses, but what will it be like this winter when there are no flowers other than the ice crystals on the windows of Doorn?" she told him.[14] Wilhelm finally said, "I don't want you to share my exile unless you know that you reciprocate my affection. I want your love, not your compassion. Don't say no! Think it over. Much is at stake for the both of us. Don't decide without serious reflection."[15]

Hermine was convinced that she would not be a good wife for the Emperor, and she knew that she could not bring all her children to live with her at Doorn. There simply wasn't room. She feared that the close proximity at Doorn would cause irritation. However, as her brain said no, her heart said yes. Hermine took three days to make her final decision. She said yes, but there would be conditions. The three youngest children would move with her to Doorn, while the oldest two would remain in school and visit them during holidays. She also maintained the right to spend 16 weeks of the year in Germany to care for the estates of her first husband. She also asked that there be no court and no court ladies. She wanted to be herself. The Emperor was glad to agree to everything as she would be sharing his exile. He could only move freely within a few miles of Doorn and needed permission from the Minister of Internal Affairs to go further. Germany was out of the question.[16] He later wrote to his friend Maximilian Egon II, Prince of Fürstenberg, "So I have found a woman's heart after all, a German princess, an adorable, clever young widow has decided to bring sunshine into my lonely house & to help share my solitude and make it beautiful with her warm, devoted love. Peace and happiness have taken possession of my torn, tormented heart now that she has given me her hand... My happiness knows no bounds."[17]

The official engagement was supposed to follow on 22 October 1922 and the Emperor wanted the wedding to take place later that same year. As an engagement gift, Hermine received a photo of his first wife. But first Hermine travelled home via Rossla where she met with her younger sister Ida. Hermine was perhaps most concerned with telling her eldest daughter

Hermine Caroline (nicknamed Carmo). Hermine Caroline had been a true daddy's girl and "clung to him with extraordinary devotion."[18] Hermine described the scene of her return to Saabor in her memoirs, "Carmo came running out of the gate of Saabor Castle to meet me. The moment she espied my face she knew that something was in the air. The sympathy between us is so great that each senses at once the slightest disturbance in the magnetic field of the other. 'Mama', she cried. 'What is it? What has happened?' I told her. Her response was at once so characteristic and so sweet that I almost burst into tears. Instead of an answer, Carmo, my shy little girl, gave me a hug that almost stunned me. 'I am glad', she cried when at last she found the words for her surging emotions. 'Now you won't have to stand alone any more. And the Emperor – how could he help loving you after he met you?' She was the only person in Germany who knew of our engagement."[19]

In early September, Hermine visited her aunt Duchess Hermine of Württemberg (born of Schaumburg-Lippe) in Regensburg to say goodbye. She then briefly stayed in Munich before accepting an invitation from her foster-mother, the Grand Duchess Luise of Baden. They spent several days together on the shores of the Bodensee. Prince Eitel Friedrich, one of her future stepsons, and Prince Friedrich Wilhelm of Prussia, a cousin of his, joined them briefly by the Bodensee. According to Hermine's memoirs, they had a heart-to-heart talk and parted as friends.

After her return to Saabor, a small airplane crashed close to the chapel where the Sunday service was being held. They had been trying to take photos of the estate. Hermine ran to help and luckily those inside had only minor injuries. The victims were an American journalist named Siegfried Dunbar Weyer and his pilot Antonius Raab. The journalist spotted a photo of the Emperor in Doorn on Hermine's piano as they waited for a doctor and he connected the dots. That very same day he cabled the news to America and it made headlines. The announcement was pushed forward, and the engagement was announced on 18 September.

Hermine gave an interview to a German journalist who described her as being, "a typical German gentlewoman. She has an energetic mouth, big brown eyes and a high forehead. There is no trace of uncertainty in her demeanour." With sadness, she spoke of her late husband. "Believe me, I have suffered immensely. For 13 years I nursed my sick husband. Day and night, I would be at his bedside in some faraway sanatorium and I did my task despite the risk of infection. Over and over again I went against the advice of his doctors. Thank God, my five children are healthy. The eldest, Hans Georg, is in Greiz in the home of the tutor who raised me, and Georg Wilhelm will join him there soon."[20]

In October, the Emperor sent Friedrich von Berg to Saabor to go over the finer details. Friedrich offered Hermine the title of Fürstin (Princess) von Liegnitz, without the Emperor's knowledge. Did he assume it would be a morganatic marriage like that of the Prussian King Frederick William II and Auguste von Harrach, who had also become Fürstin (Princess) von Liegnitz? However, as opposed to Auguste, Hermine was a Princess of the House of Reuss and was considered equal (*ebenbürtig*) to the Hohenzollern. When asked about Hermine's future title, Wilhelm answered, "Of course Empress."[21] Hermine travelled on to Greiz, where she met with her disabled brother, who showed no sign of any emotion. She spent some time in prayer at the tomb of her parents. On 22 October, she sent a wreath to be placed at the tomb of Auguste Viktoria in Potsdam.

After the engagement was announced congratulations started pouring in, including one from the Grand Duchess Luise of Baden. "That it is my dear Hermo, with whom I have always had a maternal bond, whose immensely great task it is to be able to stand by your side in the loneliness."[22] But not all were happy with the impending nuptials, including the Emperor's children. Luise wrote to the Emperor's only daughter, "I know and understand how painfully the Emperor's engagement touched his children, especially with regard to the beloved and unforgettable Empress. I am almost completely alien to you all, which of course makes the situation more difficult."[23]

Crown Princess Cecilie, the wife of Crown Prince Wilhelm, was taken by surprise by the engagement as she had known Hermine from her childhood. She challenged Hermine about why she had chosen this path. Hermine wrote to her, "I rejected the possibility of such an outcome because I did not know in advance what a deep impression the Emperor would make on me. I think we fit together and will do as much as possible to relieve him of his unspeakably hard fate. I am well aware of the seriousness of my task, which I did not choose for myself. You also kindly think of my children, I thank you very much. Certainly, it is difficult for them too, they would rather have me alone. But they love me so much that they grant me happiness. Added to this is the deep love and veneration of their Emperor and King in whom they will receive a noble and benevolent new father."[24] The Emperor was less kind when speaking of his daughter-in-law, "She (Hermine) writes to me that congratulations continue to come in, including from my daughters-in-law. They have all written kind letters, except for the Crown Princess. This doesn't surprise me at all; she has no heart, only a cold mind. She (the Crown Princess) writes about wanting to arrange authorisations. Arrange authorisations! That is the last straw! There is nothing to arrange. I can handle those things with my wife. The Crown Princess is obviously furious that she is being set aside, she wanted to play the role of Empress herself."[25]

The Crown Prince told the wife of Sigurd von Ilsemann, the Emperor's aide-de-camp, "I hope she is not marrying papa hoping to become Empress, because then it will be a very unhappy marriage."[26] She would later write, "She is not pretty in any way, has a horrible figure; she looks best in profile."[27] The Emperor complained to Sigurd von Ilsemann that General von Dommes had not congratulated him on his upcoming remarriage.[28] The Emperor's daughter Viktoria Luise was furious, not only because of the marriage but also because she had been in Doorn for two days before her father told her. The Emperor had been telling his aide-de-camp that Viktoria Luise was happy with the marriage. She told Sigurd von Ilsemann, "The fact that this woman came to Doorn with the idea of marrying the Emperor, whom she barely knew, is bad enough. Papa does not know what he is doing. His new wife will soon tire of him, of the life in Doorn and leave him. Only then will his misfortune be at the highest point and then daddy will see what mamma had meant in his life."[29] Viktoria Luise clearly thought that Hermine was a gold-digger.[30] She later wrote in her memoirs, "In the loneliness of his exile, my father took quite the understandable step. He decided to marry again. Considered from a personal point of view, it was nothing out of the ordinary that a lonely man in exile should need someone he could have permanently by his side. But for me it was very hard to contemplate another woman taking the place of our mother. In Germany the question of my father's remarriage was vigorously discussed, and there was some criticism here and there. It seemed incredible that their revered sovereign Princess should have a successor, but for my father there was no such problem. His love for his faithful wife and life-partner was unchanging, and no one could replace her, no one could put his memories of her away. He had once compared her life and her tragic fate to that of Queen Luise after the collapse of Prussia in 1807, and now that comparison was close to him personally. He remembered, too, that Friedrich Wilhelm III had married again after the death of his beloved and revered Queen."[31]

The Emperor's physician Alfred Haehner was certain that Wilhelm was making a mistake by marrying Hermine. He believed that Hermine's "sole purpose" in marrying the "elderly Kaiser" had been the expectation that the monarchy would be restored. He believed that the marriage would fail the moment that Hermine finally saw that there was no chance of the Emperor returning to the throne. "When she comes to the realisation that the game is absolutely up for her, and then considers all the things she has given up or put up with for the sake of her ambition, this will cause the marriage to fall apart. As these disappointments start to mount, her bitterness will grow, and when there is nothing left but disappointment, the bitterness will turn into hatred. This woman will never accept a life of uncomplaining resignation, she will blame the K[aiser] for the failure of her overweening ambitions... She will not allow the rift to become public... but she will increasingly leave the K[aiser] on his own, go on her travels for longer and more frequently and lead a life wholly in keeping with her own desires."[32]

Wilhelm wrote to her of his loneliness, "Lying alone and miserable in bed, a frugal pleasure which doubles the severity of loneliness, in that one lacks the true devotions of a woman who can help and making things much easier. In my despair I telegraphed old Fräulein Heym, who was nearby, to come here. She sat quietly by my bed and read aloud or knitted, and we spoke of dear old Potsdam, of Friedrich Wilhelm IV, Queen Elisabeth, great uncles Karl and Albrecht, Fritz Carl, aunts Luise and Anne, etc... with all of whom she had dealings!"[33]

Prince Oskar and Viktoria Luise wrote a letter to their father, writing about their displeasure of the upcoming marriage, which Oskar handed to him personally. They probably expected a discussion, but the Emperor did not speak to them. Instead, they received a written reply in which he wrote how sad he was that no one realised how awful life was for him in Doorn, but they would be his beloved children no matter what.[34] He wrote, "My dear children, Many thanks for yours and Sissy's (Viktoria Luise) frankness of views... I understand and respect your feelings, because I share them, and you are, and remain, my much beloved children. I do not take them amiss, for I love you too much and am so happy to have you here with me. It would be yet another pain for me if you were to turn your back on your lonely father, so there can be no question of your departure or even of shaking the dust of Doorn from your feet. I am happy at your presence here. Your sincere Papa W."[35]

Viktoria Luise learned the following month how the engagement had come about. "Princess Hermine had been widowed for two years and had five children aged between fifteen and three years. My father had hardly known the Princess and had only met her on a few occasions in peace time. When he was wondering whom to marry, he hardly knew in which way he could even meet his future bride. He was tied down in exile, but who really would come to Doorn? Princess Hermine was the first to come. One of her sons had written the Kaiser a nice, childish letter, and straight away came an invitation for him and his mother to come on a visit."[36]

The Emperor later told Sigurd von Ilsemann, "Why can't people be happy with me for my new happiness? Why can they not let anyone be happy, why must they always object? I have to keep the monarchy into account. My God, after the cruel treatment I received from the German people, I do not care! In addition, my dear Ilsemann, when one is as in love as I am, one does not know obstacles or concerns!"[37] The Emperor was convinced that by choosing a blue-blooded princess, he would satisfy the critics. The Emperor's physician Alfred Haehner wrote that by "choosing a princess undeniably of the blood" the Emperor's return to Germany was now assured. "The Princess was entitled to be and would indeed *become* the Kaiserin."[38]

The New York Times reported upon the engagement, "The ex-Kaiser's decision to remarry is a political event of importance. It has lost him the last remnants of personal popularity in Germany and given him a black eye with the staunchest Legitimists. The blindest Royalists today say that William Hohenzollern never will or can come back. More particularly has the ex-Kaiser fallen from grace in the eyes of the majority of the German women, who are even more ardent monarchists than the male reactionaries, and in those of the bulk of the monarchist-minded youth of Germany. These votaries of the Kaiserkult felt that he is not only untrue to the memory of the dead Kaiserin but untrue to their ideal of a Kaiser."[39]

Little did they know that it had been Auguste Viktoria's wish that the Emperor would remarry. The Emperor said, "The Empress discussed this at length, with the mistress of the robes, Countess von Brockdorff. When I announced my engagement to Princess Hermine, I received some abusive letters. I expected at best a coldly formal note of congratulation from Countess von Brockdorff. Much to my surprise, the old countess sent me a most warm-hearted letter, for which I shall ever be grateful. She told me that Auguste Viktoria had often discussed with her my predicament in case of her death. Almost two years before she passed away in the August of 1918, at Wilhelmshöhe, the late Empress said to her: 'My dear countess, I know I shall not live much longer. The Emperor will be alone when I close my eyes. I have only one wish – that he may soon find a wife who will love him and be good to him.'"[40]

Hermine described her four meetings with Auguste Viktoria in her memoirs. Hermine wrote, "I have already described my first meeting with Her Majesty on 8 January 1908, shortly before the severe attack of my husband, Prince Schönaich-Carolath. The occasion was a luncheon at the Imperial Palace. I remember how warmly the Empress enquired after the health of my eldest son. Hans Georg was rounding out the sixth week of his existence. Her simple words built a bridge between her and me. They conveyed to me something of the love of the Empress for her own children. [..] After my first visit to the Empress, my husband, Prince Schönaich-Carolath, hovered for years between life and death. On many occasions Her Majesty asked for a report on his health. Repeatedly she commissioned her ladies to convey to me a word of encouragement. A few years later, when the condition of the Prince enabled me to participate again, to a limited extent, in the social life of the Court, the Empress asked me for tea in her delightful salon. This was our second meeting. [...] I met the Empress for the third time at a formal Court ball – my only one. The illness of my husband, coupled with the war and the revolution, robbed me of the gay life in the capital that would have been mine under ordinary conditions. [...] My last meeting with Auguste Viktoria was one year later during the Imperial manoeuvres at Breslau in 1913. The occasion was a dinner given by the notables of the provinces of Silesia to Their Majesties, followed by a grand reception in the palace at Breslau. Here I renewed my acquaintance with the Crown Princess Cecilie, now my daughter-in-law. We had not met since we had played together as children in a small summer resort on the coast of the Baltic Sea. I have already referred to this as the last manoeuvre under the Emperor. Shortly afterwards stark realities took the place of war games. It was also my last meeting with the Kaiser until after the war. I did not meet Wilhelm II again under the German flag."[41]

To a journalist, the Emperor said, "Her Majesty the Empress Hermine, certainly lives up to my four K's (Kinder, Kirche, Küche and Kamerad – children, church, kitchen and comrade). She is the perfect mother, a perfect housewife, a devoted Christian and a matchless comrade. Her love, which led her to become my wife, saved my reason, if not my life. Accustomed to the faithful comradeship of Auguste Viktoria, I was bowed down by my terrible sorrow – sorrow for my wife, sorrow for my country. My loneliness was indescribable. It bore me down. It was hell. Now that my Hermine is with me, I have again someone to whom I can pour out my heart, who reads my thoughts and my moods." When asked about his relationship with Hermine in 1935, he replied, "I must dissemble with her as I do everyone else."[42]

He later added, "The people who criticised my remarriage

could not fathom the awful solitude that hung over my life like a pall. What do they know of my feelings? How can they realise what it means to a man, who ruled the German Empire for thirty years, to be separated from his native land by an alien border? Her Majesty, the late Empress Auguste Viktoria, was unique among women. Every drop of her blood belonged to me, to her country and to her children. Her motherly love flowed over to the cot of every wounded soldier. She was revered as a saint by my people. However, her health was frail. For years, she suffered from arterio-sclerosis. She had a stroke in the summer of 1918, long before she joined me in Amerongen."[43] He later added, "The memory of Auguste Viktoria is not a spectre dividing us, but a tie that unites us."[44] He did not always believe in this romanticised view and to a companion he confided after Auguste Viktoria's death, "I feel free at last."[45]

He also did not always have this four K's view towards women. When his first child with Auguste Viktoria was born, his mother Victoria, the Empress Friedrich, recorded, "Wilhelm is delighted that it is a boy and does not wish for girls who [sic] he considered 'no use'" When asked three years later if he would not like a daughter, he said, "girls are useless creatures; he ... far preferred to be without."[46] Women were not supposed to discuss politics or public affairs and Hermine was later known to have kept sewing materials handy so that female guests could embroider while the Emperor talked or read to them.[47]

Her youngest daughter Henriette, and her sister Ida with her husband, accompanied Hermine back to Doorn for the wedding. On the border between Germany and the Netherlands, Hermine met up with Sigurd von Ilsemann. From him, she received flowers and a letter from the Emperor. The last 150 kilometres they would travel by car and they even managed to fool the waiting press by alighting at an earlier station. Hermine and her party arrived at Doorn late in the evening. "The happy bride flew from the car into the Emperor's arms, a few intimate kisses, then she called her little daughter to meet 'Papa Kaiser'." They had a "disgusting" meal of pilau and chocolate pudding.[48]

In her new apartments, the Emperor surprised Hermine with a platinum engagement ring with a white and a grey pearl. Hermine, in turn, gave the Emperor a sapphire ring that had belonged to her father. They ate dinner in the gatehouse while her sister and brother-in-law ate with Sigurd von Ilsemann and his wife in the main house. They had a meagre meal of cooked rice and meat, with chocolate pudding to follow.[49]

In October 1922, the Emperor's daughter Viktoria Luise received an invitation for an engagement celebration and the following wedding ceremony. She recalled in her memoirs that she did not want to attend. She wrote to her father, "God willing, we are expecting a baby next spring and the journey would be difficult, so I would prefer not to undertake such a long trip. But I would, dear Papa, not be telling you the truth if I were to tell you these were the sole reasons, for it is not possible for me to let a lie come between us. I send you my warm wishes in your new life, and I beseech God that the step you are about to take will bring you what you want. But it is not possible for me to come to Doorn and take part in the wedding celebrations in the same house where mother suffered so dreadfully, and from where she departed from us. I could have no joy in a celebration such as is demanded of me. I beg you with my whole heart not to take offence at my candid words, and that you should understand my feelings fully."[50] She later wrote of her new stepmother, "My father's second wife differed in all respects from my mother, even outwardly. She was relatively small, dark and with an unprepossessing figure. She lacked my mother's goodness and her quiet ways. She was lively and industrious, like to argue, and was ambitious. Princess Hermine switched to a new existence in the life of an exile, and the quiet which had been that of the house at Doorn evaporated. Steadily and energetically the Kaiser then began to write in vindication of his policies and to counteract the propaganda picture which had been painted of him. Two volumes of memoires appeared, then a work about his ancestors, and scholarly treatises which received considerable recognition, such as Royal in Ancient Mesopotamia and Memories of Corfu. At least we saw now that Father was busy, that he had a great deal of respect for his new wife and, as time went on, we, too, managed a better relationship with her. However, I always avoided broaching delicate family affairs with her, but always in such cases she endeavoured to explain certain aspects to me. She would then tell the others after we had, just the two of us, been on a walk together: 'As usual, Sissy (Viktoria Luise) was again completely uninformed.'"[51]

Hermine had been under siege from the moment of the announcement of the engagement. The village of Doorn was overrun by foreign journalists and the amount of Dutch guards had to be increased to keep them out. One journalist even hired an airplane to attempt a landing in the park of Doorn. He was arrested and promptly deported. The Emperor was furious, "Those guys have only been writing mean things about me and now they come knocking, wanting to know things about me! I reject it all!"[52] On the day before the wedding, her sister Princess Ida had fooled the waiting press at Amersfoort station by pretending to be Hermine.[53]

On the day of the wedding itself the Emperor wore the grey uniform of a general in the First Regiment of Guards with the orange sash of the High Order of the Black Eagle. He had designed Hermine's dress himself, keeping in mind that she was a widow.[54] Hermine wore a dress of chiffon in mauve, which had been briefly detained by customs officials.[55] She described in her memoirs that she did not even remember putting it on. She wore a family heirloom emerald necklace, a stole, a black and white hat and she carried a fan with ostrich feathers. On 5 November 1922 at 11.15 in the morning, Hermine married her prince charming. Their wedding rings were plain golden bands with the inscription, "5 XI 1922 Wilhelm Doorn, Hermine Doorn." The civil wedding was performed by the mayor of Doorn, Baron A. Schimmelpenninck von der Oye. The religious ceremony followed at noon performed by Dr Vogel of the Friedenskirche in Potsdam in the main hall of the house. The reception took place in the Gobelinszimmer with a buffet lunch being served afterwards. This included salmon in aspic, ham with Cumberland sauce, chicken chaudfroid and Roman punch.[56] The black and white Hohenzollern flag flew above the house.

Of the Emperor's side of the family, only his son Crown Prince Wilhelm, his sister Viktoria, his sister Margarethe, his brother Heinrich and his sons Eitel Friedrich and August Wilhelm attended. From Hermine's side, her sister Ida attended with her husband. The regent of Hermine's brother, Prince Heinrich XXVII also attended, as head of the family. Queen Wilhelmina and Queen Mother Emma of the Netherlands both sent flower arrangements. The Emperor's brother Heinrich made the toast in name of the Imperial family, "I drink to the health of his Majesty the Emperor and King and of Her Majesty the Empress and Queen."[57]

If it wasn't clear before, Hermine was the new Empress and if the monarchy was ever going to be restored in Germany, she would be by his side. He added, "We address Kings as Your Majesty; we confer the same title upon their Queens, provided they are of equal blood. If my union with Her Majesty the Empress were morganatic, she would be merely the Princess Hermine. However, her family ranks equally with any dynasty in the world. Her late sister was the Grand Duchess of Weimar."[58] The dining room in Doorn only seated 22 people, so some of the guests were served in another room. Hermine and Wilhelm were seated on one side of the centre of the oval table. The Emperor's sister Margarethe and his son the Crown Prince sat on the opposite side facing them. On the right of Hermine was Prince Heinrich XXVII. On the left of Wilhelm was Hermine's sister Ida.

Next to Margarethe sat Prince Heinrich of Prussia. To the left of the Crown Prince was Hermine's brother-in-law, the Prince of Stolberg-Rossla. To the left of Ida sat Prince Eitel Friedrich, another one of the Emperor's sons. After the wedding, Hermine turned to Sigurd von Ilsemann and told him, "I thank you for all your love and loyalty that you have shown the Emperor so far. Now you should take a long holiday, you have not been able to take one since your honeymoon two years ago!"[59]

Meanwhile at the tomb of Auguste Viktoria in Potsdam a mysterious wreath was placed. On its pasteboard card were the words "To the silent sufferer. 5 November." The guards would later say that the wreath was left there in the early morning by one of the Emperor's sons or representatives of his sons. It was a clear indication of the feelings of the German monarchists.[60]

Some of the guests left the very same night, while others remained behind for a dinner thrown by the Count of Aldenburg-Bentinck, who owned Castle Amerongen where the Emperor had lived for the first 18 months of his exile. The wedding breakfast consisted of four courses, including roast goose and red cabbage. The Crown Prince stayed with them for ten days and he would remain a frequent guest in the years to come.

Shortly after the wedding, the Emperor conferred the Order of the Hohenzollern on Hermine's brother. The German republic was less than amused as the bestowal of orders and decorations was forbidden by the constitution of the German Republic. In addition, it was also forbidden to wear orders. It probably wouldn't matter anyway – the Prince would have nowhere to wear the order to as he rarely appeared in public at all and if he did, it was always in the company of a nurse.[61]

Not much later, newspapers reported that Wilhelm had given his wife a tiara worth several "hundreds of millions of marks."[62]

After Hermine married the Emperor, she went to Karlsruhe once more to receive the blessing of her foster-mother, the old Grand Duchess of Baden. The Grand Duchess held Hermine's hand and said, "By a good comrade to the Emperor. Stand by him faithfully. So many have deserted him. He needs your love." It was the last meeting between the two women. The Grand Duchess died in April 1923.[63] Viktoria Luise wrote, "The deaths of the older generation of the Houses of Hohenzollern and Hanover reminded us of the end of this era, too. The matriarch of our House, my great-aunt Luise, died. She was the last representative of the great old days, the daughter of the then Prince Wilhelm of Prussia, and was born during the reign of my great-great-grandfather Friedrich Wilhelm III."[64]

Chapter 5

Life with the Emperor

As the Emperor was not allowed to move around freely, a honeymoon was out of the question. They walked the edges of the perimeter but were instantly hounded by photographers and even had to be picked up by a car in one instance. The Emperor soon fell back into his daily routine of walking and chopping wood. Hermine and her new husband had breakfast together and then often went their own way. Hermine often took Henriette out on a bike.

Three decades after Hermine's death, a former member of their staff named Bart Petersen told a newspaper, "She couldn't really ride a bike. As long as she stayed in the park it was alright. If you gave her a little push as she drove off. If she had to brake, she would go into the bushes or she just dropped herself at low speed. One day I had to accompany her to Amersfoort... by bicycle. The Princess wanted to fetch her son from the train station. I feared the bicycle ride. When we got to the Amersfoortse Berg I warned her not to overdo it because she was about to flip over. It turned out alright. The Princess returned by car. The next day she called me to her. She thanked me for returning with the two bicycles, as she couldn't even ride one bicycle. When I left, she gave me two rijksdaalders (five guilders) a lot of money for that time. I thought Hermine was a nice woman, though people have different opinions about her. Perhaps it was because our birthdays were on the same day and she always gave me a present."[1]

By the afternoon they would meet again for a meal, which the Emperor followed by resting and walking. They had tea together at 5 in the afternoon, in either Hermine's salon or in the library. This was followed by reading or writing until supper was held at 8 in the evening. They often entertained guests in the evening until around 10 or 11. Because the Emperor was limited in his movements, they also organised movie nights at the house. Despite the limitations, the Emperor said, "She (Hermine) never complains; she never makes me feel that she is sacrificing herself for me. Yet her sacrifices are many, inspiring both love and respect, and deepest gratitude. She gives to her children, she gives to me; her love seems unending. It is all-encompassing, overwhelming. Our life is completely harmonious. I have never believed such perfect harmony between two human beings possible, as her fiery temperament absolutely accords with my energy and will power. I have searched history and literature without finding a parallel. We are indeed comrades in thought and aim. Her conception of life is lofty. She reminds me of one of the highly cultured Princesses of the eighteenth century, such as, for example, Queen Sophie Charlotte, grandmother of Frederick the Great, and a friend of Leibnitz, the philosopher."[2]

At the end of November 1922, Hermine's sons finally came to Doorn to celebrate Christmas with their new stepfather. New Year's Eve was also spent with the Crown Prince, his wife and their four sons. The house was getting way too small for the family and in early 1923 the nearby Orangery was renovated into guest rooms. For Christmas, the Crown Prince and his family stayed with the Count of Aldenburg-Bentinck in Amerongen. In May, Hermine had just returned from her first trip to Germany as a newly married woman and she was able to see the new rooms for herself. The German consul in Amsterdam had refused to issue a pass to Hermine with the title of Empress of Germany, and instead issued one with her former title of Princess Schönaich-Carolath. The Emperor was absolutely furious and demanded to see the consul in person.[3] When Hermine was in Berlin, she used apartments in the Old Palace at Unter den Linden 9.

The Emperor's children visited them often too and he became quite fond of Hermine's children. He later said, "I know that children by a first marriage sometimes offer serious problems. My own children frequently visit us in Doorn. Her children love me. I do not attempt to interfere between the Empress and her children. On the contrary, I hold myself aloof from the children until they come to me. I do not attempt to impose myself or my ideas upon them. I try to be merely an elder friend. Perhaps that is the reason they see a father in me. When her sons come to Doorn from school, I always feel that they are entitled to the first place in their mother's affection. Her daughters, Henriette and Carmo, bring youth and joy to my house."[4] The Emperor lovingly referred to Henriette as "The General" because she liked to dominate the household. In addition to the frequent guests, the household also consisted of the Emperor's three dachshunds, Hermine's shepherd hound Arno and Wai-Wai, a little dog belonging to Hermine's eldest daughter.

Hermine founded the Kaiserin Hermine Fund in 1922 and used it to donate 300,000 marks for hospital beds in Breslau. She also donated 50,000 marks annually to women's unions in Silesia. She was continuing her social work she had started during the First World War. This was followed in 1929 by the founding of the Hermine-Hilfswerk.

The first visit of the antagonistic Crown Princess to Doorn after the wedding came late in the year 1922. Sigurd von Ilsemann wrote down what she told him, "It was all very melancholy for me. In the old rooms belonging to the late Empress, all these images from the past came to me – and now these new circumstances and this woman in the house who is so alien to me! Hermo was kind of nice, she was very pleasant towards me, but it is all so hard for me to understand."[5] Von Ilsemann tried to talk with the Crown Princess and told her he hoped that the Emperor's other children would soon develop more understanding for the situation. Nevertheless, the Crown Princess would continue to refer to Hermine as "the new woman" and once asked Sigurd von Ilsemann, "Is it clear to the Emperor that his part in Germany is over? Won't Hermo continue to confirm the thought that there might be prospects of a return to the throne?"[6] The Crown Princess continued to enjoy a great popularity in Germany.

On the second anniversary of Auguste Viktoria's death, the Emperor held a memorial service and placed a large cross of flowers on the bed. He remained there alone for quite some time, Hermine was in Saabor at the time. He did not work in the garden that day and went out alone for a walk. Sigurd von Ilsemann wrote that he counted around 70 photos of the Emperor and his children in the room that remains unchanged.[7] Hermine once again gave an interview while in Saabor. She even had her son Hans Georg pick the journalist up from the train station. Hermine wore black as she was still in mourning for Grand Duchess Luise of Baden. The journalist asked about her marriage and she answered, "I can only say that we are very happy. My children love the Emperor very much and the Emperor loves my children, like they were his own. At Christmas, they were all in Doorn, along with the Crown Prince and Crown Princess and their children. There was an atmosphere of kind understanding between us." She also spoke of the rather monotonous days at the house. "In Doorn the day starts in the morning with a silent practice of religion. After that the incoming mail and the work in the house and garden is done. The afternoon meal is as simple as possible and a comparison with a regular German civilian family would put Doorn to shame. In the afternoon and in the evening, we read and write a lot. It is a shame we do not have the opportunity to make music."[8]

Hermine returned home early upon the urgent requests of her husband and came to Doorn in time for Pentecost. She was picked up from the train station by her stepson the Crown Prince. Due to some miscommunication the Emperor awaited Hermine's car at another location, to the great amusement of the Crown Prince. Despite the jokes, the Crown Prince and Hermine had had a serious conversation about the fact that the Crown

Prince had spoken negatively about his father in public. For once Sigurd von Ilsemann agreed with Hermine and he informed the Crown Prince that the Dutch people had been most affected by the way he spoke of his father. The Crown Prince said, "Papa does think he is still popular in Germany. But the people just laugh and mock the Lord of Doorn. His mistake is mainly that he does not think about the people, but only of himself. I do not trust Hermo on this point either. No doubt she still has hope for the throne as well."[9]

By early June, Hermine confined to Sigurd von Ilsemann how unhappy she felt in Doorn and that she blamed the Crown Prince and his interfering in matters that did not concern him. According to her, he mocked his father and enjoyed making funny faces while doing it. Hermine accused the Crown Prince of being a coward and of being unmanly.[10] She regretted returning to Doorn early and her children had blamed her for it. She feared that she would always be followed by the Emperor's sad letters whenever she left. She had also not been treated well in Germany. Several gentlemen had turned their backs on her, but she refused to tell the Emperor. Perhaps she had begun to realise the implications of her marriage and the impossibility of the Emperor ever returning to the throne.[11]

Maybe she had also realised that the Emperor was not quite the prince charming she was expecting. "The strongest man, in certain moods, is only an overgrown boy. Emperors are no exception. What a big baby the Emperor is! What sort of crimes have been committed against the poor man over the years, and how badly his first wife handled him! Now it is certainly too late, Oh, it is really difficult!"[12] Even the Emperor's physician Alfred Haehner recorded, "It was at times really sad to see and to hear how sharply critical they both were of one another. From her (he means Viktoria Luise who had come for a visit in August) father's letters she had expected to find joyous happiness and total harmony... She was... painfully disappointed at what she found here. Her father had gone ahead and taken the step she would never be able to condone, but in spite of all that she had hoped that things would turn out well. But that was not at all her impression and her heart was very heavy indeed." Reportedly, Hermine told Haehner, "Perhaps it would have been better if I had not remarried at all!"[13]

He commented, "There was quite a strong undertone of bitterness in her words, it appears that she only now realised what a burden she has taken on when she took this step. It may well be that her ambition to 'play at being a Majesty' presented itself in such a brilliant light that she completely failed to see the dark shadows. For she must surely realise that the K[aiser] will never again play any part in politics and being addressed and treated as 'Her Majestät' by this little circle here has lost the attraction of novelty. She now sees only the hard life ahead, the isolation, the loss of personal freedom. Someone with her character will not come to terms with that but will on the contrary grow ever more bitter. How will it all end? Certainly not well."[14]

Crown Prince Georg of Saxony came by for a visit in September and Sigurd von Ilsemann recorded that he had very few good things to say about Hermine.[15] Later that month, the Emperor's physician, who had come to check up on a sick Sigurd von Ilsemann, told him that he believed that Hermine had only married the Emperor out of ambition. According to Sigurd von Ilsemann she had been nervous and irritable all summer and the situation would not improve in the following months.[16]

In the spring of 1924, Hermine suddenly became very ill and was in bed for weeks. The New York Times reported that Hermine was suffering from articular rheumatism combined with a high fever and a weak heart.[17] The doctor recommended that she would need to go to Baden-Baden for a cure. For this particular trip, she was accompanied by the Emperor's youngest sister, Princess Margarethe.[18] It was the start of many years of taking the cure at spas and she continued to have health problems from angina, to stomach issues and virus infections. When she underwent an operation in Germany in 1937, a relieved Wilhelm wrote to her, "God has blessed our marriage and he has given you back to me!"[19] Nevertheless, her frequent absences and trips were immediately causing rumours of marital discord.[20] Hermine commented on the rumours in a letter to Sylvia Cushman, "I was very much amused to hear that we two are not divorced, but separated. If the people knew how well we get on together, what a charging father he (the Emperor) is to my beloved children, they would not write or believe such rubbish. I enclose a little photograph taken on our Sunday walk – I think it is so sweet."[21] It was looking like things were becoming more settled and Hermine had come to terms with the situation.

In addition to her new life in the Netherlands, Hermine often returned to Schloss Saabor, where she had books in cases stacked all the way to the ceiling. She must have been devastated when she lost all 19,000 volumes during the Second World War. The Emperor was quite proud of Hermine's intellect, saying, "I know of no other German woman possessing the intellectual discrimination of Empress Hermine. She is the friend of poets, writers and artists. Her library is immense. There are probably few women in the world who can boast of such a library. In addition to her splendid library in Doorn, she has large collections of rare books in Saabor, the castle she inherited from her first husband."[22] He added, "The Empress has many contacts with intellectuals. She never hesitates to state her point of view. She is ever ready to take up the cudgels for me. I mention the incident of the German professor (who had written a book about the Emperor without meeting with him) only to point out how Her Majesty the Empress is fighting my battles like a true wife and a true comrade, because she understands me. She fights more loyally for me than many of my subjects ever did. Yet her reward – in Germany, at least – has been ingratitude and vilification. However, lies, as we Germans say, have short legs."[23] To the end of her life, she continued to read and was most interested in history, specifically the First World War.

It was perhaps no surprise then that Hermine would set out to write her own memoirs. *Days in Doorn* was released in 1927, just five years after she married the Emperor. Despite her love of books, Hermine wrote, "I have no favourite author. Life immediate reflection – biography and memoirs – interests me most of all. I am fascinated by psychological novels. But I am equally attracted by descriptions of countries and peoples. Geography intrigues me. Now that I am unable to travel much, I dote on reading about the travel of authors. My favourite book remains Rudolf Schott's *Indian Voyage*. Whenever I am tired or annoyed, I delve into its pages. This immediately restores my equanimity. Perhaps the book pleases me because it reminds me of happy Italian days when I first caught glimpse of eternal beauty. It is no affection to say that I prefer records of travel and discovery to fiction. Reading enabled me to keep in close contact with the world, even if my wings are clipped by my exile."[24]

In May 1924, Hermine returned to Germany with Henriette. The Emperor continued to chop wood in the park to the unhappiness of the gardener as the wood could not be used during that time of year.[25] One of the members of Hermine's company wrote in August from Baden-Baden that everyone in the hotel was very excited about having her stay there, despite the fact that she did not engage with other people much.[26] Hermine spoke with a "socialist" during her stay there, who published an article saying that if Hermine had been by the Emperor's side during the revolution, the outcome would have been different. Naturally, this pleased the Emperor to no end.[27] In late September, Hermine met with Crown Prince Rupprecht of Bavaria in Berchtesgaden and wrote to the Emperor ensuring him that he still had the Bavarian Crown Prince on his side.[28] Hermine began to make it her business to see the Emperor return to Germany, though the Emperor himself was unsure if he wanted to live in a republic. On her return to Doorn, Hermine stopped in Hanover to speak with Field Marshall Paul von Hindenburg, but the visit was unsuccessful as he continually tried to avoid even making eye contact with her.[29]

In March 1925, Hermine was once again ill, and she underwent an operation in Berlin. Newspapers reported that she had a benign mass removed from a muscle and that the operation went well.[30] She was being treated by "a famous female doctor" and stayed in bed for about 14 days.[31] On her way back to Doorn, Hermine stopped in Charlottenburg and Potsdam to visit the graves of several members of the Imperial family.[32]

In May 1925, the Duke of Saxe-Coburg and Gotha, who had also abdicated in 1918, and his wife Viktoria Adelheid (born of Schleswig-Holstein) visited the Dutch court but when they were ordered to return to Germany before visiting Doorn, so that it would not appear that they came straight from the Dutch court, the Emperor was outraged. He told Sigurd von Ilsemann, "This is unheard of and I won't let it go. I have sent Berg (Friedrich Berg was the Chief Representative of the House of Hohenzollern) to The Hague immediately to make some noise. It's been seven years and it has to end. Those people should be happy that I continue to stay in the background." Hermine was quite excited about meeting the ducal couple and their 17-year-old daughter Sibylla, who would become the mother of the current King of Sweden.[33] Despite the outburst, the Emperor and Hermine visited Queen Emma of the Netherlands at Soestdijk Palace at the end of the month.[34]

In July, the Emperor, Hermine, Prince Oskar and the visiting former King Friedrich August III of Saxony travelled from Doorn to the Castle of Middachten in De Steeg. They were also joined by the Count of Aldenburg-Bentinck and three of Hermine's children. According to newspaper reports, the visit was a friendly one and they stayed until the evening before returning via Arnhem.[35] At the end of 1925 came the news that German republicans were demanding the prosecution of Hermine for using the title of "Queen." The use of titles was no longer allowed in Germany and Hermine had visited hotels and signed the guestbooks with "Kaiserin" and "Queen." It all came to nothing however as prosecuting officials could not find sufficient reason for a suit.[36]

In early 1926, the talk in Doorn had returned to the days of November 1918. The Emperor told Sigurd von Ilsemann, "From a reliable source I now know that Hindenburg bitterly regrets not arresting Groener, Hintze and the others and instead advising me to go to the Netherlands. Despite this, people still say that I fled out of cowardice! I thought I could trust my advisers, I thought I was dealing with people that I could trust."[37] In May, Hermine left for Germany for three weeks and the Emperor continued to rant to Sigurd von Ilsemann.

In June, Sigurd von Ilsemann recorded a very unpleasant conversation with Hermine as they walked in the garden. "First we spoke of how dignified the Emperor carried his heavy fate. She asked me if I truly believed that it had been God's will and if that thought helped the Emperor. She did not believe it. 'With religious matters His Majesty is often a mystery to me. His comments do not always match with how he acts.' Then she became very agitated and added, 'Nobody takes me into account. When the Prince of Waldeck (brother of Queen Mother Emma of the Netherlands) was over for dinner the day before yesterday, the Emperor kept saying, 'My wife' and he means his late wife! I am his wife and when he speaks of the other one, he should say 'My deceased wife' or 'My late wife' or something like that. But he doesn't even think about it!' She began to shake all over, stomped her feet and waved her arms as she shouted at me, 'For four years I have been his wife. I am the Empress and I only have the right to the title!' When I tried to calm her down and told her that the Emperor had not intended to hurt her, she answered, 'What I have done, nobody thanks me for it. I would like to meet the woman to take over this self-sacrificing task in Doorn as I have done. And who thanks me for it? Why do none of the gentlemen say anything to His Majesty when he speaks of his wife and the Empress and means the deceased Empress. Because they are all cowards, nobody has the courage! I keep asking something for everyone else but nothing for myself, no I am too proud! The only one who would do it is Nitz. He is the only one who is there for me. If I asked him, he would go to the Emperor straight away.' The poor woman was so worked up that she began to cry. She was shaking and kept screaming louder. I said nothing because she would only go against me. This truly unpleasant conversation ended upstairs by the door. 'My services are not recognised by anyone but maybe someone will see it after my death. That I need to vent after being treated such will surprise no one.' Then the Empress shook my hand and disappeared!"[38] Disappointment was clearly setting in.

In August of that year, newspapers reported that Hermine was being sued by a speech therapist from Dresden named Muller who had treated her son Prince Ferdinand Johann for four months. The article stated that Hermine thought the bill too high and she had refused to pay. In 1925, the 12-year-old Prince Ferdinand Johann had undergone surgery with a "nerve-doctor" and was also suffering from a speech impediment. The doctor had then advised Hermine to hire Miss Muller, who managed to cure the speech impediment. Afterwards the speech therapist asked for 2400 marks, while Hermine thought that 1250 marks was plenty. Miss Muller initially wrote to Doorn but was again refused.[39] The court case was delayed and eventually the court ruled in Hermine's favour.[40]

In May 1927, it became clear that the Emperor would not be allowed to return to Germany, and he issued an order for all the gentlemen who carried his medals and wanted to visit Doorn to leave the German National People's Party. If they didn't follow the order, they would need to return the medals.[41] The order was, of course, unworkable, though the Emperor did not seem to realise this. At the end of May, Hermine once again travelled to Germany. This time it would be for ten days only. When she returned, she brought all her children, except for Georg Wilhelm. In November, Hermine had lost Georg Wilhelm in an accident. She mentions the accident surprisingly briefly in her memoirs saying only, "The Fates have not always dealt kindly with me, but they even up all the scores when they gave me my children – three sons and two daughters. Alas, they deprived me of Georg Wilhelm, my second son, as he was blossoming into manhood. An accident ended his promising life in the fall of 1927."[42] The New York Times reported, "Prince Georg Wilhelm zu Schönaich-Carolath, second son of Princess Hermine, present wife of the former Kaiser, died this morning in the City Hospital at Grünberg, Silesia, from injuries received in a motorcycle accident on Sunday. The Prince, who was 18 years old, was thrown from his motorcycle. He was brought to the hospital last night unconscious. Physicians found he had a fractured skull and internal injuries, but an immediate operation failed to save him and he died without regaining consciousness. His mother received the news of his death while en route to Saabor, the Silesian family seat of Schönaich-Carolath."[43] On 4 November 1927, he was interred at Saabor. Hermine attended the funeral alongside the Crown Prince and Crown Princess, Prince Oskar, Prince Ferdinand Johann and the Grand Duchess of Saxe-Weimar (born Princess Feodora of Saxe-Meiningen).[44]

It was not the only tragedy in 1927. The House Reuss of Greiz became extinct upon the death of her brother in October of 1927. The New York Times reported, "Prince Henry XXIV, the last male representative of the former Sovereign House of Reuss under the older line and a brother of Princess Hermine, the present wife of the former Kaiser, died here (Gera) today at the age of 50. He was the son of Prince Henry XXII, the last ruler of the Principality of Reuss and an implacable opponent of Prussia. Though a physical giant and handsome in his younger years, the dead Prince had been an idiot since childhood because of an accident. Repeated operations failed to restore his mentality."[45] A Dutch newspaper stated that the cause of death was pneumonia.[46] Surprisingly, Sigurd von Ilsemann makes no mention of either event in his diaries.

The following May, Hermine left for Kissingen and according to Sigurd von Ilsemann, it was wholly a propaganda trip. In the hotel in Leipzig where she would spend the night, 35 people were invited. An employee of the hotel said, "How is she going to speak to so many people in just two hours? With that 'high woman' everything goes *en masse*: letters, humans and books!"[47] Whenever she left Doorn, she wrote to the Emperor on a daily basis and sent telegrams along the way. He, in turn, often wrote back twice a day.

In early 1929, Hermine came down with rubella. Sigurd von Ilsemann was delighted because this meant that she would not be able to attend the Emperor's 70th birthday activities. He wrote, "A cloudless sky, winter weather and sunshine!"[48] The Emperor himself was not quite as happy, "That my wife should be ill at this moment, when she would be able to take her rightful place in the family for the first time!" One of the Emperor's sons commented, "Fate has intervened and has knocked out the Schönaich-Carolath family, who do not belong here. This is a curious turn of events."[49]

A huge 'W' was set up over a baldachin and fireworks were set off. The number of guests was a logistical nightmare because the house was so small. The Count of Aldenburg-Bentinck took in several guests at Amerongen, but others found a place to stay in Hotel Cecil or in the nearby Driebergen or Zeist. A new medal was struck for the Emperor and guests were entertained with footage of the Emperor touring the front.[50] In Hermine's absence, the Emperor's daughter Viktoria Luise acted as hostess. The former King of Saxony toasted the Emperor's health in front of 70 guests around 12 tables.[51]

The year 1929 was all about a curious court case involving a man named Karl Hartung who claimed to be Hermine and the Emperor's illegitimate son. He had apparently defrauded several people for substantial amounts. He also presented himself as Hermine's secretary to gain people's trust. After earning their trust, he borrowed amounts of money which they never saw again. Hartung was also being prosecuted for having published several untrue news articles in a newspaper. He had falsified a letter that was supposedly from Hermine and started with "My dear boy" and was signed with "Your mother Hermine."[52] Hartung was sentenced to a year and one month in prison.[53] He appealed the decision and he claimed to have received several payments from Hermine. The court case was delayed after it was initially decided that Hermine should be interviewed.[54] Hermine then admitted that she had supported Hartung and had received him in Saabor. She claimed that when she found out he was a fraud that she had ended all contact.[55] Karl Hartung was initially released but was again convicted in 1933.[56]

There are just two public letters of Hermine in the Dutch Royal Archives in The Hague and one of them dates from 4 January 1930. It was written to Queen Emma and reads,

"Dear, honoured aunt,

At the beginning of the year, I send you my warmest and most sincere blessings, and I would like it to bring you and your family only good!

On the 2nd of January, Count Lynden was here and told me about his conversation with you, which somewhat removed the bitterness that had arisen in my heart. You will understand that I am so deeply impressed with what Wilhelm is doing and what he must suffer and endure, that he must feel deeply and so I keep from him what is not necessary for him to know.

My eldest daughter got the measles for the second time this year, while she was with friends in Germany, she was missing for my birthday, at Christmas and New Year, and can only return on the 16th. I hope that she will be better here on the 27th and in February back in Germany with acquaintances, since I cannot carry through the whole situation, and we will have a nice, sociable winter. It's so hard to do justice to everyone with a shared heart, but I am glad that I'm not useless in the world.

Convinced that you will understand me in everything, and thankful for your ever-shown goodness, I am in sincere reverence,

Your ever-true niece. Hermo."[57]

In June 1930, the inhabitants of House Doorn celebrated the 25th wedding anniversary of the Crown Prince and Crown Princess. On Sunday the 8th of June, the silver couple arrived with three of their sons – Prince Ludwig Ferdinand was in Argentina – and both of their daughters at Amersfoort train station. Several of the Crown Prince's brothers also came with their wives and children. The Emperor's daughter and her husband also came, as did the Grand Duke and Grand Duchess of Mecklenburg-Schwerin and their sons. The celebrations began with a church service on Monday as flowers began to be delivered to the house. The family had lunch together and gave gifts to the couple. Afterwards some of the family members went out for a walk. In the evening, there was a banquet and a movie night. Newspapers reported that the celebrations went on until very late in the evening.[58] Later that month, the Emperor and Hermine went out sailing with Catalina von Pannwitz when a nearby boat suffered a fire in its carburettor. The boat with the Emperor immediately sailed to help the stricken boat where one of the women had suffered very serious burns. Luckily there were no fatalities.[59]

Hermine's travels to Germany also meant that, during the rise of the Nazi Party in Germany, she came in contact with Adolf Hitler himself. In early 1930, Sigurd von Ilsemann recorded a conversation with the Emperor's fourth son, August Wilhelm. The Prince told him that he knew that Hermine hated him, especially since Nuremberg last summer when she had shown up at a party thrown by Hitler without being invited. She had asked Hitler if he could take the Emperor and herself back to Germany, but he said that he could not.[60] She also attended the Nuremburg Rally in 1929. August Wilhelm had joined the NSDAP (National Socialist German Workers' Party) on 1 April 1930, to the horror of his father. The Emperor had written to his son, not only immediately demanding his leaving the party, but saying that there would be consequences if there were "unpleasant consequences" due to his membership.[61] The NSDAP won 18% of the votes in the election of 1930 and August Wilhelm must have been happy to have joined.

Magnus von Levetzow, German Rear Admiral and politician wrote to Hermine, "I would like to be able to tell your majesty about patriotic things occasionally. Today I just want to mention that lately I have personally approached Hi. (Hitler)."[62] She wrote back, "...to be able to see and speak in detail anywhere the many plans and thoughts that we cherish together... it is my pleasure to be able to have a little bit of cooperation with your trust."[63] It was also von Levetzow who arranged for Hermann Göring to visit Doorn in 1931 and 1932. Göring was enlisted by Hitler to court potential supporters from the ranks of princes and the aristocracy. It certainly helped that his wife Carin was a Swedish born aristocrat.[64]

To cover up the visit in 1931, Hermann Göring's wife was also invited and they were signed up under the name Döhring.[65] They visited on 18 and 19 January 1931 and Hermine was quite excited about it all. The Emperor and Göring had spent the time discussing matters and the Emperor had tried to impress him. On the first night, the Emperor had stood up and toasted to the "coming empire." According to Sigurd von Ilsemann, Göring believed that the Emperor should return to the throne, but the other German monarchs should definitely not. The Emperor did not agree with this at all.[66] Göring's wife Carin recalled after this visit that the two men "had flown at one another... Both are excitable and so like each other in many ways. The Kaiser has probably never heard anybody express an opinion other than his own, and it was a bit too much for him sometimes."[67] Hermine made sure to serve impressive food – pheasant with cauliflower, Viennese roast, roast goose and snails.[68] Viktoria Luise wrote in her memoirs, "Hitler also tried to make contact with my father and sent Hermann Goering to Doorn. As a famous Luftwaffe pilot of the First World War and decorated with Germany's highest military honour, Pour le mérite, Hitler considered him a suitable spokesman. He was quickly disillusioned. The Kaiser received Goering coldly and somewhat angrily, since the man's crude and outspoken manner clashed brusquely with the more staid customs of the Court."[69]

Prince August Wilhelm was furious that he was not the one who had brought Göring to Doorn. Hitler had written the Prince a letter that he was supposed to pass to his father, but he refused to do this. Hermine was most impressed by Göring and called him "a loyal and decent man", even though this had been their first meeting.[70] She even "pressed a wad of banknotes" on Göring, presumably to help pay for a cure for the very ill Carin.[71] Carin died in October 1931.

There was considerable hope that Hitler, once risen to power, would be in favour of restoring the monarchy. The rest of the family remained quite surprised that both the Emperor and Hermine seemed to believe that a restoration was possible. Their belief came up again when the Crown Prince's eldest son, another Wilhelm, wished to marry Dorothea von Salviati, who was not of equal birth. Prince Wilhelm wished to give up his rights to the throne to marry but as he was considered to be a future Emperor, the Emperor was quite against it. In April 1931, Prince Wilhelm visited his grandfather in Doorn, and they talked for 30 minutes. He told his grandson, "Remember, there is every possible form of horse. We are thoroughbreds, however, and when we conclude a marriage such as with Fräulein von Salviati, it produces mongrels, and that cannot be allowed to happen."[72] Prince Wilhelm left feeling dejected and unsure of what to do. General von Dommes told Prince Wilhelm that he would destroy any chance of a restoration with this marriage. Although Prince Wilhelm initially decided against marrying Dorothea, they eventually married in 1933.[73] Hermine was reportedly more open minded about the whole thing and said, "If they are smart, they will marry straight away in Bonn."[74]

On 18 November 1931, an intimate dinner with Hermine, Hitler and Göring in the salon of Baroness von Tiele-Winckler was arranged. She managed to charm Hitler and he was impressed by her commitment. He presented himself to Hermine as the saviour of the nation. Hermine did not leave until 1 in the morning, bedazzled by Hitler. "Hermine was so impressed by Hitler's well-informed opinion of the problems that afflicted Germany, by his enthusiasm and his ideas for solutions, that she was beginning to support the idea of a meeting between Hitler and the Emperor at Doorn." It was von Levetzow who urged the Emperor to join forces with the National Socialist movement and von Levetzow was elected to the Reichstag for the NSDAP in 1932. Hermine was naïve to believe that Hitler had no other goal than to help Germany. However, the Emperor had come to realise that Hitler was never going to share power. Shortly after the November meeting, Hermine went to the theatre with some of her children and members of her household. Heavy security was needed at the entrances to prevent anti-royalist demonstrations. She also visited a charity bazaar.[75] In 1931 and 1932, the Emperor's sister Margarethe and her husband Friedrich Karl also had "Herr Hitler at Kronberg for tea."[76] Around

Christmas 1931, Doorn was buzzing with the possibility that the Emperor was being restored. Sigurd von Ilsemann wrote, "All hopes, all thoughts, all conversations and all letters are based on this belief." They believed it would only be a matter of time before Hitler himself visited Doorn.[77]

On 19 May 1932, Göring once again visited Doorn and he met with the Emperor as he was chopping wood. Hermine accidently walked by during this meeting and she tried to leave but the Emperor called her to him. Göring stayed for several days, had tea with them and walked with the Emperor. To Sigurd von Ilsemann the whole situation was very surreal and he could not believe that they were putting their faith in the Nazis. The next goal was now to get Hitler to Doorn. With renewed energy the Emperor began to think about how he would organise the military. In October 1932, the Crown Prince had written a letter to his father, to which the Emperor had replied with criticism about the Nazis. This letter had ended up with Göring somehow and it finally led to the Emperor realising that the Nazis did not have his best interests at heart. Hermine believed that is was the Crown Princess who had sabotaged the letter. The situation led to some tense scenes in the house with the staff standing around huddled in groups as Hermine raged. Sigurd von Ilsemann wrote, "Her Majesty has again shown how dangerous she is."[78] At the end of the year, the Emperor became ill and for Hermine it appeared to have been a breaking point. She said to Sigurd von Ilsemann, "It was inevitable that the Emperor would become ill! You have no idea what goes on in the Emperor's head. You don't know what that poor man is going through. I am his wife and his only confidant. I only know what is going on in his head. Do you hear me? Or do you have another opinion? I have my dear children and they will help me. Won't you, my dear boys? 'Yes, mama, of course', Hans Georg answered. It all came out so shakily, half-crying, with fits and knocks, so full of blame over the lips of this nasty woman that I thought an explosion was going to happen. All her hate towards me was glowing in her eyes and I thank my own calm attitude and silence that she did not attack me. Who knows what the unsuspecting Emperor told her to get her in such a prickly mood? She is probably angry that I spent so much time at the bedside of our highborn patient, but she doesn't have to worry. None of our conversations are about her."[79]

In June and September 1932, Hermine and the Emperor ventured out of Doorn together and visited the seaside town of Zandvoort. The day before their departure in September, Queen Emma visited them at Doorn.[80] They were photographed in Zandvoort and it shows the Emperor wearing a raincoat and cap, while Hermine wore a sensible suit. A newspaper reported, "The former Emperor of Germany and his wife and her children left on Tuesday morning around half past 9 in two cars for Zandvoort. As far as is known the former Imperial family will remain in Zandvoort for the entire week."[81] Indeed, the court marshal reported to the police commissioner in Zandvoort, "It is my honour to tell you that their Majesties the Emperor and the Empress intend to take a day trip to Zandvoort in good weather on Friday the 8th of September. The Majesties would come to Zandvoort at about 11am and have their midday meal at the house of Freiherr von der Heydt. The return to House Doorn would presumably start after the tea." However, when the weather turned out to be nice, the couple intended to stay for a few more days in the house of Freiherr von der Heydt, which the court marshal duly reported as Wilhelm needed permission to venture outside of Doorn. Wilhelm was no stranger to the Dutch seaside; he had visited Scheveningen as a child.[82]

In late September 1932, Hermine was back in Berlin and Bella Fromm, a Jewish aristocrat, recorded in her diary, "Whenever 'Empress Hermine,' Kaiser Wilhelm's second wife – the Quotation Mark Empress," as Conny von Frankenberg calls her – comes to the capital, she attends one of the Countess von der

Groeben's Sunday afternoon receptions. This time the hostess, who is eighty-five years old, gave her 'imperial' guest a slight inkling of what was in her mind. She said in her impeccably courteous and grand manner: "Your Majesty, I have been told that your sympathies are with the National Socialists. Is it true that His Majesty has made a donation to the National Socialists? Hermine stood there in embarrassed silence."[83]

In December, the same Bella Fromm recorded, "The 'Empress' had some one hundred thirty guests for tea today at her charity bazaar. Regret about the lost monarchy was frankly stated. Hermine had a rather superior smile on her lips, almost smug. The Doorn household has no doubt that Hitler is going to smooth the path for the Hohenzollern restoration. 'Her Majesty' received in black velvet, lavishly trimmed with lace. It trickled down her back on a background of pink chiffon. I was careful to avoid the customary hand kiss when my turn came, as her white kid gloves looked by that time like an ordnance map in white and red from the lipstick of those who kissed before."[84]

By the end of 1932, the rise of the Nazis had torn the family apart. The Emperor had violent arguments with his sons and even with his stepson Hans Georg. He demanded that they all leave the Nazi party. Hans Georg had been attacked on a train for wearing a swastika and was escorted off the train and back to Doorn after calling his assailants "a bunch of Jews."[85] Security had been tightened around House Doorn for the celebration of Hermine's birthday that year when a man made an attempt on the Emperor's life on the 12th of December. An unknown German man climbed over the fence of the park and managed to get into the house and into the tower room, which bordered the Emperor's study. He was found there by servants who immediately called for assistance and they managed to overpower him. He had a knife and revolver with him and apparently intended to kill the Emperor. At the request of the German authorities, the man was deported to Germany and his identity could finally be confirmed as Heinricht Fuecker. He later claimed that he had not intended to hurt the Emperor and had simply wanted to hand him a letter. He had brought the weapons to defend himself. The German authorities questioned him as well but agreed that the man had wanted to kill the Emperor.[86] The following Christmas, the Emperor was ill with a cold, leaving Hermine to preside over the Christmas celebrations herself.

In early 1933, Hermine travelled to Berlin and she wrote to her husband that the situation there was much changed. She was in her element there and had spoken with many political leaders. Newspapers immediately began to speculate that Hermine intended to meet with Adolf Hitler, even though the journey had been planned to open a charity bazaar.[87] On 22 February 1933, Hermine indeed met Adolf Hitler. Sefton Delmer, correspondent of the British newspaper Daily Express wrote about the meeting.

"Empress Hermine, a stately, self-confident lady – she was the extraordinarily wealthy second wife of the Emperor – arrived in Berlin fourteen days after her husband's former corporal had taken power. She expressed the wish to speak to him straight away. But Hitler avoided her.

The Vice Chancellor of Paper, on the other hand, paid her respects on Sunday, February 19, as the faithful monarchist he was, gallant to the empress, and told her that he would do everything in his power to make the restoration of the Hohenzollern his priority. Still, however, the omnipotent Hitler refused to meet with Hermine when Frau Victoria von Dirksen, the stepmother of one of Hitler's most distinguished ambassadors and at the same time one of the most brilliant hostesses in Berlin, had a great idea. After all, she was both true to the Empress and Hitler. She wanted to give a big evening party and invited both of them.

Right at eight o'clock on February 22, 1933, the guests gathered in the von Dirksen house in the Margretenstrasse

- very close to my apartment. Ten minutes after eight, Hermine appeared. She was of the opinion that Herr Hitler was expecting her here together with the other guests, just as it would be fitting for Princes to visit their subjects. But Mr. Hitler was not there. Frau von Dirksen's beautiful 17th century English clock struck the quarter of an hour - then the half hour. Poor Hermine! Would he come? Was he not coming?

A quarter to nine, Hitler entered the room without a word of apology. He looked like the director of a provincial circus with his tuxedo, white bandage, and carefully trimmed forelock. Frau von Dirksen was faced with a difficult protocol question: Should she introduce the Empress to the Chancellor or the Chancellor to the Empress? Hitler solved the problem for her. He stepped elegantly up to Hermine, clicked the heels of his patent leather shoes, bowed stiffly and said: 'Hitler!'

'Heil Hitler! Mr. Hitler!' Hermione replied nervously as the Führer gallantly kissed her hand. During the meal, Hermione had no opportunity to speak to Adolf for herself and for her cause. The two sat at the opposite ends of the table. After dinner, however, she managed to get him involved in a conversation.

And what did Hitler say to her when she said that it was time to do something to reintroduce the monarchy, or at least to allow the emperor to return to his homeland? 'I would be proud if I could contribute something to the return of your noble family to their legally appropriate place,' said Hitler. 'No one is more aware of the great merit that the House of Hohenzollern has acquired for the Fatherland, but unfortunately the time is not ripe, in the present moment such a measure will provoke only unrest and turmoil, this attitude we have to take into account in our delicate situation today, has by no means welcomed a sweep of this kind. I can tell Your Imperial Majesty in the strictest confidence that an exceptionally important English agent will inform me even before we have taken the government that the English government has been most concerned about any attempt to reintroduce the monarchy in Germany.'

At that moment, Victoria von Dirksen saved both her Empress and her Führer from further embarrassment. I heard the story that same night from one of von Dirksen's guests. My newspaper put it on the front page the next morning. And so, it came about that the Berliners first learned from London that the Empress had been amongst them."[88]

After the meeting, newspapers immediately jumped on the story.[89]

She was still in Berlin when the Reichstag building was set on fire and claimed that her life and that of the Emperor's sons had been in danger. The following Reichstag Fire Decree of 28 February suspended basic rights and allowed detention without trial. Just a few days later, the NSDAP managed to get 43.9 percent of the votes during the election. Hermine believed that the monarchist movement was making progress and she returned from Berlin a happy woman. Reportedly, Nazi-leader Ernst Röhm had said to expect a monarchy by the autumn. In April, Sigurd von Ilsemann wrote that Hermine had totally turned the Emperor to the Nazi cause. Around this time, Prince Wilhelm had written to his grandfather about his marriage to Dorothea von Salviati. He had come to realise that she was definitely the woman for him and that no one was going to stop him from marrying her. "Wilhelm is damaging the monarchist movement with this engagement, just as it's making progress," the Emperor said. He immediately sent General von Dommes to Bonn in an attempt to change the Prince's mind.[90] However, his mind could not be changed. On 5 May 1933, Bella Fromm recorded in her diary, "Today I met Prince Wilhelm, the eldest son of the Crown Prince. He is engaged to be married to Dorothea von Salviati from Bonn. 'Grandfather and my parents were mad at me. But I shall marry her anyway,' he said. 'I renounce my rights. You know, Grandfather really lives in the illusion that the Nazis are going to restore our throne!'"[91] When the wedding day was upon them, Count Finckenstein told Sigurd von Ilsemann, "Today is the day that Prince Wilhelm smears the Hohenzollern race and breaks the principle of legitimacy."[92]

Meanwhile the Emperor confided in Sigurd von Ilsemann about Hermine, "My wife's barometer is stuck on storm again. She is in an unbearable state. Politically, she means well. My return to the throne cannot happen fast enough for her but we won't get there with her way. She follows the Nazis and does all she can in Berlin, and in writing from here, which does more damage than good. I try to give her a good example with my reserved attitude. I'll have them come to me. I will not follow those people. If I am ever able to take up the reins of government again, then providence will take care of it. For that we must now wait with calm, dignity and reservedness. Her Majesty says that it is my fault that we have not gotten any further, because I let Kleist and von Levetzow go. Through them I had the necessary contact with the Nazis. Well, thanks for that. What has von Levetzow done in those five years? Absolutely nothing, despite the enormous sums I paid him. And Kleist, what has he done? He brought the second man of the Nazis, Göring, here and he behaved rudely too! Yes, it is sad that Her Majesty is making my life so difficult. I truly have enough worries as it is!"[93]

During the summer, Hermine travelled back and forth to Germany. She wrote back to Doorn that she wanted some sign of confidence in Hitler from the Emperor. Hermine and Hitler met by accident when Hermine was visiting a friend in Berlin. She wrote back that she found Hitler "a well-raised and nice man."[94] She returned to Doorn on 9 August 1933 and to the horror of Sigurd von Ilsemann this also meant the end of the peace and silence for when Hermine was home, there was always a coming and going of guests. The Emperor remained wary of the Nazis and he would often rage after reading the speeches that were being given as none of them mentioned him. He began to regret that he had not forbidden his son Prince August Wilhelm to work with the Nazis.[95] According to Hermine, Hitler had told her that she was the only one he could trust in the House of Hohenzollern.[96] Sometime during the summer of 1933, an agreement was signed by Göring in his capacity as Prussian Minister President and Friedrich von Berg, who represented the House of Hohenzollern. From then on, "The Kaiser, the Crown Prince and the remaining Prussian princes received a substantial allowance from the Prussian state." Reportedly, a condition of the agreement was that the Hohenzollerns pledged not to publicly criticise Hitler or the Nazis. Meanwhile, the Emperor's porcelain factory, which he still owned, was doing good business turning out busts of Hitler.[97] Hitler sent mixed messages about his willingness to restore the monarchy during his quest for power. He told General von Dommes in April 1934, "If Germany were ever again to become a monarchy, then this ... must have its roots in the nation – it must be born in the party, which is the nation." Later he said, "He had not made the November revolution (the overthrow of the Emperor), but it had done a good thing in ridding Germany of the princes."[98]

The Emperor's nephew Philipp, the son of his sister Margarethe, later the Head of the House of Hesse, was an ardent Nazi supporter and in his quest to secure his relationship with his uncle, he made him godfather of his son Heinrich and he also paid regular visits to Doorn. Nevertheless, he seemed more interested in National Socialism than the restoration of the monarchy. He continued to forge close ties with the Hitler regime even after Hitler definitely closed the door on a restoration.[99] He later said, "I always had access to Hitler if I wanted it. I was rejected only once in a while. Unfortunately, I had no influence in a political sense. Where I had influence, it was very slight. I can only say, that Hitler evinced a benevolent attitude – except a few times – and remained that way."[100] The chief denazification board judge said after the war that their relationship was characterised as, "of a special kind... Although not a true 'National Socialist' in the narrow and real sense – as both Philipp and Hitler recognised, there was a special political trust and human benevolence on the part of Hitler that ostensibly went so far that the Prince von Hessen was for years perhaps the only German – notwithstanding very few exceptional cases – who had access to Hitler at any time. And this at a time (before and after the unleashing of the war) when many Reich Ministers had to wait six to nine months before they were permitted an audience."[101]

The Emperor's daughter Viktoria Luise and her husband also met Hitler several times and discussed, "a rapprochement between England and Germany."[102] Of their first meeting, Viktoria Luise wrote, "I first met Hitler in 1933, when he invited my husband and me for talks in Berlin. The fact that it was Joachim von Ribbentrop, at that time Hitler's foreign affairs adviser, who had issued the invitation, showed on what basis the talks would be held. We were to discuss Anglo-German relations. Hitler appeared extraordinarily polite, was very correct, and spoke in friendly fashion."[103] A short while later, she wrote in her memoirs, "It was after this sojourn in England (1934-1935) that we received an astounding demand from Hitler, conveyed to us by von Ribbentrop. It was no more or less than we should arrange a marriage between Friederike (their daughter) and the Prince of Wales (the future King Edward VIII). My husband and I were shattered. Something like this had never entered our minds, not even for a reconciliation with England. Before the First World War it had been suggested that I should marry my cousin (the Prince of Wales), who was two years younger, and it was now being indicated that my daughter should marry him. We told Hitler that in our opinion the great difference in age between the Prince of Wales and Friederike alone precluded such a project, and that we were not prepared to put any such pressure on our daughter."[104]

At the end of 1933, as Hermine returned from a few days in Berlin, she once again had a serious conversation with Sigurd von Ilsemann. The Crown Prince had told her that "one of the gentlemen in Doorn" had accused her of politically influencing the Emperor and she had wanted to know if von Ilsemann was that gentleman. He had to assure her several times that it had not been him. She then told him that she did not agree with the Emperor's stance that the Crown Prince should not wear the swastika armband with the uniform of the Hussars. The Emperor was becoming even more disappointed in his wife's stance on the Nazis. "Her Majesty considers everyone who does not think like her about the Nazis as her enemy."[105] The tensions in Doorn were becoming unbearable.

The year 1934 did not begin much better. Hermine verbally attacked a visiting woman who had criticised the fact that Hitler was spending 19 million to rebuild the stadium. Apparently, it was such an awful a scene that the Emperor nearly had a heart attack.[106]

The Emperor's 75th birthday festivities lasted for four days. There were several royal guests, including the former King of Saxony. The Emperor seemed to particularly enjoy the presence of his grandchildren. Sigurd von Ilsemann spoke with several members of the family about the rise of the Nazis and he commented that one appeared in favour, while others were against them. The newly married Prince Wilhelm was not present and had written his grandfather a short note, "I ask you to accept my congratulations for the 27th. I hope that everything you wish for this in this new year of life will come true."[107]

Hermine made sure that firewood and other provisions were distributed among the citizens of Doorn for the Emperor's birthday.[108] Just after the occasion, Göring had proposed to disband all monarchist organisations in Germany. "On 30 January, General Göring, in his capacity as chief of the secret police (of Prussia), proposed to the Minister of the Interior that all monarchical associations should be dissolved, and on 2 February Dr Frick requested the State governments to dissolve and forbid all such bodies immediately."[109] The Depute Gauleiter in Berlin, Arthur Görlitzer, noted, "We deprecate the action of the gentleman in Doorn in writing letters telling people to get busy and see to it that Germany again becomes really happy by a return to the monarchy. We will treat people who indulge in these activities exactly as we treat those who think they ought to do propaganda for Moscow. For they are even more dangerous than the latter, because they approach intellectual circles and so deprive us of the men we need to help us."[110]

The Emperor had received the proposal and had read part of Hitler's recent speech. According to Sigurd von Ilsemann, the Emperor was quite calm and reasonable.[111] He later commented, "The Empress keeps looking for people to blame and accused me of careless statements that led to the Nazis stance on the monarchy. However, they have been anti-monarchist from the beginning. In hindsight, I am glad that I stuck to my opinion about the Nazis, though others have continually tried to convince me that Hitler and his people are monarchists. They have all fallen for it. The women are the most excited about the Nazis. They cannot be convinced, and people should let it rest!"[112]

At the end of February, Hermine wished to travel to Berlin but for the first time in years, she worried that the city might be unsafe. The Nazis were not happy with her doing politics and she feared that she might be arrested if she went there. She then showed the Emperor a picture of the Crown Prince in his SA (Sturmabteilung)-uniform. She told her husband, "Two years ago your son said that all Nazis should be hanged and now he is one of them!"[113] The Emperor was furious and told Sigurd von Ilsemann, "One could not think this is possible! I told the Crown

Prince that I would consider him an enemy of this house if he put on this uniform! He looks like a cop!"[114] The Emperor sent General von Dommes to Berlin to speak to the Crown Prince and according to Sigurd von Ilsemann, Hermine cut the words *Greizer-Zeitung* from the photo so that he would not know that the photo came from her. He believed it to be all part of her plan to set father against son. However, the greatest irony was that both of Hermine's surviving sons had joined the Nazi party.

In May 1934, Hermine was still gushing about Hitler. In a letter to a friend she wrote, "May Hitler succeed in all his great plans... It always touches me to the heart... that he wants and strives for the goals which the Kaiser instinctively and fervently pursued but was prevented from attaining by those working with Him and by His reactionaries who boycotted and watered them down. From the bottom of my soul I wish Hitler complete success in the great things he is planning!"[115]

In June, Hermine and the Emperor met with Randolph Churchill, the son of Sir Winston Churchill, in Arnhem. Randolph Churchill was then invited to breakfast in Doorn. Randolph Churchill was a journalist who wished to write an article about the Emperor, but the meeting did not go well. Hermine said, "This young Englishman was not very respectful to the Emperor. He asked the most unbelievable questions. He also hated Germany and he called Hitler names. When I asked why he had supported the restoration of the monarchy just a year ago, he answered that he was still for it but only on a completely democratic basis. No, I did not like this man at all."[116] Nevertheless, Churchill was kindly received an hour after Hermine's rant. Perhaps the couple had expected more but Churchill was clearly there as a journalist. His article appeared in the Daily Mail on 11 June.

In early July, the house was buzzing with the news of the Night of the Long Knives. During this night, several political extrajudicial executions took place intended to consolidate Hitler's hold on power. The Emperor was most indignant about the way Ernst Röhm and his wife had been executed without a trial. Hermine was reportedly less indignant, and she had said that the events of 9 November 1918 might have gone differently if several officers had acted the way Hitler had acted now. Hermine was still determined to go to Germany and when she was assured of police protection, she left for Berlin with her two daughters. They did not return until the middle of August. During her absence President von Hindenburg died at the age of 86. The Emperor refused to hang the flag at half-mast as he did not consider him to be a Head of State. Newspapers later reported that Colonel Reinhard, the leader of the Kyffhäuserbund, an organization for War Veterans, had claimed at von Hindenburg's memorial service that von Hindenburg had not advised the Emperor to go into exile in the Netherlands. Sigurd von Ilsemann surmised the angry letter that Hermine wrote him, "Why did you do this? A justification of Hindenburg, honoured by every Germany anyway, at the expense of the abandoned and lonely Emperor. That does nobody any good and it was not necessary because the Field Marshal has been in the spotlight for years while the Emperor has been in the shadow. I don't need to tell you about the services that the Emperor has done for the army and the world war, although they appear to have been completely forgotten. The Emperor could not know that all the messages that reached him in Spa were based on lies and deceit and that so many at home and at the front were still loyal to him. Hindenburg confirmed to me in 1925 that he told the Emperor to go to the Netherlands. He said that it was a necessary step and that is why he gave the Emperor that advice. Why must you, while you were there on 9 November 1918 in Spa, deny this now and put the Emperor, who sacrificed himself with the best of intentions and betrayed by the home front and advised as such, in a bad light? I cannot believe that you have truly said this? This is either very indiscreet or a very mean dig. May I ask you to tell me who is responsible for this publication? With this matter the poor Emperor has been given another dose of poison."[117] With the passing of the "Law Concerning the Highest State Office of the Reich" the day before von Hindenburg's death, Hitler could no longer be removed from power. Despite this, the Emperor did not believe that national socialism would last.

In addition, several articles appeared in newspapers reporting on the Emperor's financial difficulties. The household often bought items in bulk in Germany but the situation was not exactly stable. Around 60 members of the staff at House Doorn had their wages lowered.[118] At the end of the year, both Hermine and Princess Juliana, later Queen Juliana of the Netherlands, donated a doll for an exhibition.[119] She also opened a charity bazaar as part of the Hermine-Hilfswerk in Berlin. She took along her daughter Princess Henriette and her step-daughter-in-law Ina Marie, the wife of Prince Oskar.[120] Her presence at the bazaar was openly mocked by the national socialistic press in the "Angriff" (literally translated as "attack") magazine, which was set up by Joseph Goebbels. They wrote, "Mother of the country Hermine has arrived from Doorn in Berlin to open the Hermine-Hilfswerk. The *Lokal-Anzeiger* (a Berlin newspaper) has sent a photographer there to capture this world historical event. And we see Empress Hermine next to Princess Oskar of Prussia (Ina Marie) and Princess Henriette, her daughter. And we see how the Empress bends over horses, birds, vases and porcelain plates, which will defeat the distress of the winter. Hermine-Hilfswerk: To see, it is not a joke, in the Herman Göringstrasse, the very highest circles of society, moral conscience, aid relief. Hermine-Hilfswerk – for ladies and gentlemen who feel so very lost and passed over by love in their great aide work, for ladies and gentlemen who wish to confirm their great attachment to the 'court' in Holland with money."[121]

The relationship between the Dutch royal family and the German Emperor in exile and Hermine had its ups and downs. Queen Wilhelmina never visited Amerongen or Doorn and it wasn't until 1927 that she gave her husband permission to visit them. Prince Hendrik (born of Mecklenburg-Schwerin) and the Emperor mostly spoke of military matters. Prince Hendrik found it easier to see Wilhelm's side of the story as his family too had lost land in 1918 and had been left basically penniless. Hendrik himself lost part of his income and then he also had to assist several of his family members.

Queen Wilhelmina's mother Queen Emma did visit Doorn several times. When a memorial service was held on the first anniversary of Queen Emma's death, Hermine sent a wreath.[122] In 1935, Hermine had attempted to arrange a match for the unmarried Princess Juliana. This apparently happened upon the request of the Princess's father, Prince Hendrik, without the knowledge and against the wishes of Juliana and her mother Queen Wilhelmina. In October, Prince Bernhard of Lippe-Biesterfeld had visited Doorn – who called Hermine "Aunt Hermo" – for the second time but Queen Wilhelmina would have none of it. Two years earlier she had already written to Hermine, "I am unpleasantly surprised to find that her Majesty the Empress has made several attempts to seek a possible marriage for Princess Juliana. Her Majesty the Queen asks Her Majesty the Empress to abstain from any future steps."[123] Even Prince Bernhard's mother Armgard had visited Doorn in 1935 and was reportedly in correspondence with Hermine and Wilhelm.[124] Hermine continued her matchmaking and later asked Princess Elisabeth of Stolberg-Rossla, who had married two of Prince Hendrik's brothers in succession, to recommend Prince Bernhard.[125] Prince Bernhard did end up marrying the Princess in 1937 after finally meeting her at the 1936 Winter Olympics. On 2 June 1937, Prince Bernhard visited the Emperor at House Doorn, and the Emperor returned the favour on 21 June when he visited Soestdijk Palace. Hermine joined him for a visit on June 1938[126] to congratulate Princess Juliana and Prince Bernhard personally on the birth of Princess Beatrix and again on 21 May

1939, when they drank tea and watched movies.[127]

At the Emperor's 76th birthday in 1935 an "incident" took place. Although exact details are not given, the newspapers reported that a chef had acted in a "fit of rage." The man was apparently arrested and immediately sent to Germany where he was admitted to an insane asylum. The Emperor was said to be quite taken aback and Hermine was quoted as saying, "If people knew what this man had intended to do, he would surely be condemned to death."[128] Then Hermine's secretary Georg Martin Wunderlich reportedly quit his job or was fired by Hermine after nine years because he wished to marry Hermine's daughter Caroline. Newspapers reported that the family was against the match but Caroline herself was in love and was even taking cooking lessons.[129] The engagement is not reported upon again, though Caroline did end up marrying a commoner the following year.

At the end of 1935, Bella Fromm once again wrote about Hermine in her diary. On 6 December, she recorded, "'Empress' Hermine, during one of her stopovers in Berlin, invited, once again, some hundred and fifty guests to the Niederlaendische Palais. There is always the same routine. In the vast entrance hall, two tottering old castellans with snow-white hair sit behind huge antique desks. They give the pen, with shaking hands, to each guest, who has to enter his name, address, and a telephone number in one of the two guest lists. Another ancient castellan ushers the properly listed guest inside. The chamberlain on duty introduces each newcomer. Then follows the serving of refreshments, the gossip, the tepid piano recital. Last night, everything went according to schedule – inside. A little surprise upset the routine in the hall when the Gestapo appeared and confiscated the guest lists. The castellans were frightened and bullied into silence. The 'imperial' receptions don't last late into the night. I was back home and asleep when the doorbell rang: the chamberlain on duty had found out what had happened.

Hurriedly, he gathered five young noblemen. Furnishing them with names and addresses of tonight's guests, he sent them on a round of warning. I went downstairs to unlock the door. Young von Troelsch, after a hasty side glance, slipped in and reported what had happened. 'You'll know how to act gnädige Frau (Madam)' Did I know! The ever-ready emergency suitcase in my hand, I jumped into my car and drove out into the country. There I propose to stay until I get a hint that the danger is over."[130]

Hermine wrote at the end of 1935 praising Hitler, "One's heart leaps when one thinks of what the Führer has again given Germany this past year – universal military service!" She added, "God preserve this man whose aims are so very pure!"[131] To an officer she wrote, "We are all so proud of our new army – what an achievement by the Führer, what a leap over the ditch of the Treaty of Versailles!"[132] She later wrote to British General Wallscourt Hely-Hutchinson Waters, "Of course, I feel in my heart and for the Kaiser the great strain that another man – not he himself can rule Germany – but I am thankful to Hitler and glad for Germany that after all these disgraceful years since 1918 to 1933 a man stood up and saved Germany from shame, slavery, death. England may not repeat 1914 – may not treat Hitler as it treated my poor Kaiser."[133] When Hitler backed Franco's fascism with military support, Hermine wrote to Waters again, "The Kaiser is exceptionally pleased at our intervention against Spain, against the red tide and at our combination with Japan against Bolshevism. England's behaviour is incomprehensible; the awful thing is that it will not only be England but Europe which will suffer if the red flood is not stemmed in time. What madness and what blindness!"[134]

In early 1936, Hermine was once again in Germany. She wrote to her husband about wanting to come back sooner but for the first time he wrote back to her that she did not need to hurry. According to Sigurd von Ilsemann, she was "following around Nazi leaders without informing her husband."[135] She had also managed to secure lunch with Göring, but he had stood her up. Hermine tried to send her husband the headlines by highlighting the news that she considered important. However, the Emperor took up reading, or rather listening to someone read to him, the Evening Standard, instead of just the German newspapers.[136] In late 1936, the impending wedding between Hermine's eldest daughter Hermine Caroline and a commoner named Hugo Herbert Hartung was announced. He was an employee of Leuna works.[137] Hermine's response to her new son-in-law is not recorded. The civil wedding ceremony took place at Wilmersdorf on 10 December with a Lutheran service following at Schloss Saabor two days later. There were only two witnesses to the ceremony, the bride's eldest brother and the groom's father. Nevertheless, a large crowd had gathered outside the city hall to shower flowers on the newlyweds.[138] Hartung was imprisoned by the Russians during the Second World War and was killed on 31 December 1945.

Early in 1937, Walter Krivitsky, a Soviet intelligence officer who later defected and was found dead in 1941, sent a man named Paul Wöhl "unofficially" to approach the Emperor in Doorn and to suggest that, if the Reichswehr officers visiting him in great numbers could be counted upon, the Hohenzollerns might be restored to the throne. Wöhl never saw the Emperor, probably because he was ill with the flu, but he did see Hermine who liked the idea. We don't know if the Emperor ever knew of the plan, but the plans were taken to the top of Soviet intelligence. Nikolai Yezhov, a Soviet secret police official, took the idea to Joseph Stalin himself. He later reported that Stalin had pointed at a map of Western Europe and indicated how much closer London was to Doorn than was Moscow. "If the British don't try," said Stalin, "they must have convincing reasons." And so, Walter Krivitsky's plan to undermine Hitler died an early death.[139]

In March 1937, Bella Fromm last recorded Hermine in her diary, though it was rather more about Hermine's son who had brought a woman to the Turkish Embassy Ball. She wrote, "Something of a scandal was caused by Prince Carolath, son of 'Empress' Hermine, who brought his lovely blonde mistress to the Turkish Embassy Ball. It came out that she was a salesgirl, and there were lots of shocked complaints. The Prince was entirely unruffled. 'Why not?' he demanded with charming arrogance. 'Society is full of important Nazis who drag along, legally, ex-cooks, seamstresses and shop girls.'"[140]

In August, the Emperor and Hermine undertook a small outing when they went to visit Twickel Castle in Delden. Newspapers reported, "Accompanied by his wife, Princess Hermine, and his entourage, the former Emperor of Germany arrived at Twickel Castle this afternoon just before half past twelve. A small group of people awaited the arriving grey Mercedes-Benz car, with the guests, and a following car. When the cars arrived at the castle, they took off their hats and the former Emperor acknowledged this with a friendly nod. The guests were received on the terrace by the castle's inhabitants, Baroness Van Heeckeren tot Wassenaar – born Countess Bentinck. Also present for the greetings was the hostess' sister, who was living at 'Weldam'. The former Emperor, dressed in a light grey overcoat with a flat cap, also engaged two foresters who had formed a guard of honour. The guests returned to House Doorn at 4.30."[141]

In September 1937, the New York Times reported that Hermine had undergone a "serious operation" in Potsdam.[142] A second article in October clarified that Hermine had had an appendectomy. She returned to Doorn in October after visiting the north of Italy to recover.[143] For a short time it appeared that Hermine was seriously ill, and the Emperor intended to travel to Germany to see her and had even arranged it with the Nazi government. They had agreed to him visiting only on the condition that he would return to Doorn immediately after the visit. Fortunately, it was not necessary.[144] Later that year, Hermine's daughter Henriette fell ill with measles and had to be nursed away from Doorn.[145]

When the future Queen Beatrix of the Netherlands was born in early 1938, Doorn was in a celebratory mood. The Emperor and Hermine sent a telegram to the Dutch royal family and had the traditional "beschuit met muisjes" (aniseed rusk covered with a sugared and coloured outer layer, which is blue for the birth of a boy and pink for the birth of a daughter) sent to their staff.[146]

The annexation of Austria in early 1938 baffled the Emperor. He told Sigurd von Ilsemann over and over again, "I do not understand what is happening!"[147] Just three hours from the Emperor's place of exile, the last Austrian Empress and her son waited to be restored to the throne, which would never happen. Hermine was happy with the events and wrote, "How swift at just the right moment and how terribly audaciously the matter has been handled."[148]

Hermine was in Germany when the Emperor suddenly fell ill in March. He later said, "It was horrible that I suddenly could not breathe. I thought I was over and done with!" It was an angina attack and although Hermine was immediately informed, she was also firmly told to stay put. She had been ordered to rest by her doctor after feeling run-down.[149] Hermine obliged and telephoned later that evening to inquire after her husband's health. A few days, he again felt unwell and the doctor felt unable to leave as the Emperor might need him at any moment. Despite feeling unwell, he remained in high spirits. Hermine remained worried about him and returned to Doorn in early April. The political turmoil continued to fascinate the Emperor. At the end of the month, he and Hermine once again visited Zandvoort and Hermine stayed a few days longer than he did.[150]

The year 1938 also saw the wedding of Prince Ludwig Ferdinand, second son of the Crown Prince, and Grand Duchess Kira Kirillovna of Russia, daughter of Grand Duke Kirill Vladimirovich of Russia, head of the House of Romanov, and

Princess Viktoria Melita of Saxe-Coburg and Gotha at Doorn. Bella Fromm recorded on 8 January 1938, "'Prince Ludwig Ferdinand is engaged to be married to the Russian heiress to the throne, Princess Kyra!' gossiped Brandenstein. A proper royal match! They still seem to think the Nazis are going to put them back!"[151] The New York Times reported, "Despite the civil marriage and Orthodox Church consecration in Potsdam yesterday, Prince Ludwig Ferdinand of Prussia and Grand Duchess Kira of Russia are still considered unmarried, according to the austere Lutheran views of the head of the Hohenzollerns family, whose family members gathered here today. The marriage will be consecrated once more at noon tomorrow by Pastor Doering, the former Kaiser Wilhelm's court chaplain. Most of the party present at Potsdam yesterday arrived in the Netherlands this morning in two special railroad cars and were welcomed at the station by the Governor of the Province of Utrecht, representing Queen Wilhelmina. The former Kaiser, awaiting his guests at the main entrance of his residence, was visibly moved when a huge grey automobile halted and one after another his five sons stepped out, followed by their wives, children, a few old friends and members of the Romanoff family, and then his favourite grandson with his bride, who, although smiling happily, looked nervous."[152] The couple was married in the private chapel at Doorn and Princess Juliana was among the guests as well.

In July, Hermine ventured out of Doorn again to visit the Centraal Museum in Utrecht to visit an exhibition on ancient art. She was received by the mayor and received a private tour from the director of the museum.[153] The following month, Hermine was back in Germany and she attended the wedding of her step-granddaughter Princess Herzeleide, the only daughter of Prince Oskar and Ina Marie. She married Karl Biron, Prince von Courland in the garrison church at Potsdam.[154] When she was back in the Netherlands in September, Hermine and the Emperor were allowed to travel to Amsterdam where they visited the

Stedelijk Museum which had an exhibition on treasures from the antiquity.[155] Hermine briefly returned to Germany after this to visit family but was back in the Netherlands by the middle of October.[156] At the end of November, she joined the Crown Prince for yet another visit to Germany, but she was back home in time for her own birthday.[157]

The Emperor's 80th birthday was celebrated with around 50 guests. Several of them slept in the house but others had to find accommodation in hotels in the neighbourhood. The day itself started with a religious service, as was usual. Prince Bernhard joined the Emperor for lunch as did a representative of the Dutch Queen. After the banquet, the movie "Der Choral von Leuthen" (The Hymn of Leuthen) about Frederick the Great was shown.[158] From the citizens of Doorn, the Emperor received a new garden house.[159] Viktoria Luise wrote of her father's birthday, "My father's eightieth birthday on 27 January 1939 was the next occasion for a family celebration. He was supremely happy to have such a huge gathering about him to pay him honour, especially when so many friends of his had already died, and many of the Generals who had been so close to him had been recalled to that great Army in the beyond. The events in Germany had done more than enough to turn attention in a direction other than Doorn, and he was not unaware of this fact, but he did not complain. But now and then he would let slip a word or two which indicated how he felt. [...] Among the guests at Doorn were Crown Prince Rupprecht of Bavaria, Grand Duke Friedrich Franz of Mecklenburg, the Margrave of Meissen, Grand Duke Vladimir of Russia, and Crown Prince Paul of Greece. Naturally, his children and grandchildren were there, too, as was Prince Bernhard of the Netherlands, who brought him the Queen of Holland's good wishes. Field Marshal von Mackensen, the Kaiser's faithful old friend, was there. It was ten years since I had seen him last, and it was very pleasant to see him and the Kaiser sitting together, and, like old veterans, talking of the past."[160] King George VI of the United Kingdom also sent "his heartiest congratulations."[161]

In April 1939, Hermine was warned by Hermann Brüning that soon the Netherlands would be invaded by Germany.[162] The Netherlands had begun to mobilise as the situation in Europe deteriorated. In the middle of April, Prince Ludwig Ferdinand and his young wife Kira arrived with their two-month-old baby son Friedrich Wilhelm. While Ludwig Ferdinand only stayed for a few days, Kira stayed for several weeks.[163] Princess Juliana was asked to be godmother and although the baptism had taken place in Potsdam before they came to Doorn it was expected that Juliana was going to visit them. On 27 April, Princess Juliana indeed took her family to House Doorn. As she arrived, she held up the one-year-old Beatrix to the window. They stayed until 6 o'clock.[164]

The following month, Hermine's son Hans Georg became engaged to Baroness Sibylle von Zedlitz und Leipe to the joy of both the Emperor and Hermine.[165] Dutch newspaper *De Telegraaf* posted a profile of Hermine during this time. It read, "At House Doorn an exile lives. Once Emperor, always a controversial figure, now an old man, who kills his time with fads and the truly excessive interest of the sober Dutch. Foreign countries don't have him so realistically near and romanticises his exile and follows his comings and goings with an often sickly interest."

"By his side a woman lives – not an Empress, people call her Princess Hermine; she married the Emperor in his exile. She does not have the heavy burden of a romantic past and so remains in the shadows of the unknown next to the figure who often has the spotlight of international interest on him. M.G. Schenk visited her at House Doorn and gives us the following description in 'The Lady and her House': "The Empress is young, despite her grey but carefully dressed hair. Her clothes are very simple. She apologizes for wearing a blouse and a skirt, but she finds them most comfortable to ride her bike in and she enjoys riding her bike on Sunday afternoon, like this Ascension Day. A pearl necklace falls over a high closed white silk blouse. As soon as she sits down, she takes her embroidery, puts on her spotless white gloves and embroiders further on a gobelin pillow that will be brought to her 'store' to be sold for charity. 'I always continue working during conversations to keep my supply up. Even when the Emperor reads to me at night, I have my work. He reads to me a lot.'"

The story goes on about her charity until Hermine shows the reporter some of her books. "In the hallway there are tables full of books about various subjects. A few days ago, a book was published on Franco-Spain, it is present here and lies brotherly next to a book on Soviet Russia. A bright swastika sticks out against a white sheet where *Mein Kampf* lies; next to it is a brand-new book about Ukraine. There are novels, there are academic books."[166] For the rest of the year, newspaper articles were scarce.

In October 1939, Hermine wrote to her friend Max Buchner, "The Kaiser and I are watching all these great events unfold from the bottom of our hearts and are proud of our troops. God bless Germany. How wisely has the Führer and those who have not deserted him, those who kept faith with him, the civilians and the military, arranged and achieved everything – how great is the unity. If only all those involved in 1914-1918 had done their duty in the same way, we would never have had a 1918. I believe I can say in all honesty that the Kaiser and I are delighted from the bottom of our hearts that the Führer has not had to confront the difficulties which the Kaiser experienced both militarily and at home, and during the war as well, alongside all his great concerns for the war and the Fatherland."[167] To her sister-in-law Margrethe she wrote in December, "How fabulous are our achievements, especially at sea and in the air! Wilhelm is so proud of it all and is totally absorbed by these great events!"[168] In another letter a few days later she wrote, "We do not doubt that he (Hitler) will succeed in bringing perfidious England to its knees and to conquer for Germany the place in the sun which it needs and deserves. With all our thoughts and wishes we are back home and at the fronts where such great things are being achieved. The Kaiser is proud of the young Wehrmacht and delighted at all the blows raining down on England."[169]

In early 1940, the Count of Aldenburg-Bentinck, who had welcomed the Emperor into his home in 1918, died. Hermine personally brought flowers and a letter of condolence from the Emperor, who apologised for not being able to be present due to a cold. During the funeral he was represented by General van Dommes.[170] The Emperor's birthday passed in silence, though Princess Juliana and Prince Bernhard did send flowers. Very few family members were present.[171]

On 10 May 1940, Germany indeed invaded the Netherlands and Doorn was right in the centre of the battle. Sigurd von Ilsemann, who was officially no longer in the Emperor's service, wrote that day, "From 3.30 a.m. one can hear heavy shooting. Hundreds of planes are flying from Germany along the Rhine in the direction of Rotterdam. Arrived at Doorn at 5 a.m.. Everything is still quiet. A little after 7, Colonel van Houten appeared and says that he has been ordered by the commanding General that all of the staff of House Doorn is to be interned. Only few are allowed to stay here. By 10, most were returning. It became clear later that returning had been a mistake. Their Majesties were allowed to keep seven persons in their staff. All others were told to come outside around 5 in the afternoon with their luggage and they were to be interned outside of Doorn. Colonel van Houten has taken the responsibility in keeping more staff than what was originally ordered. Those who were left behind had to sign a statement saying that they would not leave the park or do anything directly or indirectly against the Dutch state. In the morning and the afternoon His Majesty takes me for a walk in the park. In the afternoon and the evening, a common meal. Late in the afternoon Count Schwerin arrives from the hospital.

The Dutch staff was also ordered to leave House Doorn, save for two men and a woman. All the gates and fences are closed with chains. The field wardens stay, as they were before, guarding the main gate."[172]

Just two days after the invasion, Hermine and the Emperor received an offer from the British government to stay in England for the duration of the war as Doorn would soon be a warzone. One of Winston Churchill's secretaries wrote to the Foreign Office, "Mr Churchill wonders whether it would not be a good thing to give the ex-Kaiser a private hint that he would be received with consideration and dignity in England should he desire to seek asylum here."[173] The Emperor was adamant that he would not leave. "No, whatever may come, I will not leave Doorn House!"[174] He also said he "would rather be shot in Holland than flee to England. He had no desire to be photographed beside Churchill."[175] Queen Wilhelmina never visited the Emperor while he lived in Doorn but she did offer him a stay on a Dutch island if he desired.[176] The Emperor responded, "I am deeply grateful for your offers, but I shall not be able to take advantage of it as I am looking forward to meeting my destiny here where I am living."[177] The fighting would continue for the next few days and Sigurd von Ilsemann recorded Dutch troops passing through Doorn.

A little before 8 in the morning of 14 May, the first German troops arrived at the gates of Doorn and they were immediately let in. Hermine welcome the regimental commander Colonel Neidholdt and some of his officers. A message from Hitler promised that the Emperor was to be protected by the German army and he promised that the house and the estate would not be occupied by the Germans. On 21 May 1940, General von Dommes issued the following statement, "Should there be any entry into Holland by the Germans in the course of the war, His Majesty has laid down the following guidelines: 1. He will desist from what could malevolently be represented as flight. 2. He does not wish to claim the hospitality of any enemy of Germany." It followed, "The swift commencement of a state of hostilities does not make it possible for the Kaiser to join the German troops. Doorn, as is known, lies between the two Dutch defence lines, and the Dutch government has advised His Majesty on many occasions that in the event of war he should seek a place not directly in the battle zones. The Kaiser, nevertheless, has decided to remain in Doorn. On the outbreak of hostilities His Majesty, together with Her Majesty, Princess Henriette and their closest entourage, as well as some of their personnel, were interned in Doorn. The greater part of their personnel has been transferred to an internment camp in Northern Holland. As all radio sets had to be surrendered immediately, House Doorn was completely cut off from the world. The only news which reaches Doorn tells of the failure of German attacks in Northern France and Belgium and the successful resistance to the Germans in Holland. In Doorn one experiences air raids and alarms. At midday on Whit-Sunday Baron Nagell, the mayor of Doorn, appeared before His Majesty with an offer from the British Government. In view of the old family relationships and the Kaiser's dangerous situation in the war zone, the British Government offered him asylum in England. His Majesty, understandably, refused."[178]

Hermine wrote to her sister-in-law Margarethe, "It would have been quite grotesque for us to go over to the enemy and besides a satiric drama if we had then to meet with the Queen of this country who has always slighted us here. I must say that Wilhelm has not been treated by any important German authority since 1918 with anything even remotely like the respect now being shown him by our gracious Führer."[179]

Hermine was delighted by the arrival of the German soldiers and wrote to Catalina von Pannwitz, "The first German soldier in front of the steps to the house was such an incredible relief that I cannot find words to describe it. I shall never forget the expression on the Kaiser's face as he stood on the steps together with the commanding officer of a regiment – suddenly he was 30 years younger." To her stepdaughter Viktoria Luise she wrote, "You won't believe how He has been rejuvenated by all these events and how delighted He is that the Dutch pressure has been lifted from Him. At times he has the bearing he had 18 years ago. Every soldier He sees brings Him the greatest joy, and the news is playing its part in making Him proud and happy."[180]

On 23 May 1940, the Emperor's grandson, Prince Wilhelm, who had married against the Emperor's wishes, was shot during the French campaign and died of his injuries. Some 50,000 people came to mourn at his funeral, which disturbed Hitler. He then decided to stop any of the princes from serving at the front.[181] Despite this personal tragedy, the German advances excited the Emperor.

He was placed under the protection of the Wehrmacht, though this soon turned from protecting to guarding. It took great convincing to get the Emperor to send Hitler a congratulatory telegram.[182] "Deeply impressed by the truce with France, I congratulate you and the entire German army with the God-given amazing victory with the words of Emperor Wilhelm the Great: 'What a turn of events through God's dispensation!' All German hearts are filled with the chorale of Leuthen, which the victors of (the battle of) Leuthen, the soldiers of the Great King sang: Now thank we all our God! Wilhelm I.R. 17 June 1940."[183]

In August 1940, the Emperor announced the betrothal of his grandson Prince Karl Franz Joseph of Prussia, the eldest son of Emperor's youngest son Prince Joachim of Prussia and Princess Marie-Auguste of Anhalt, and Hermine's daughter Princess Henriette. According to a newspaper article, Hermine sent a telegram to Adolf Hitler to announce the betrothal on 19 August. She wrote, "In the midst of this great event the fate of the one is not so important. Yet, I would like to announce the engagement of my youngest daughter Henriette to Prince Franz Joseph of Prussia, who during the hard days of war has stayed with us bravely and faithfully and who joined us in our indescribable joy and relief at the invading and victorious troops. He held his own and hopes to cooperate and fight along with them. We hope, wish and trust that the final, decisive battle against England will succeed and that all your far-reaching and glorious plans will be realised. Full of pride we keep our eyes focused on everything that takes place in the heimat (homeland) and on the fronts. Your dedicated Hermine."[184] The betrothal reportedly took place "without festivities" at Doorn.[185] They were married on 1 October 1940 in a civil ceremony there. For the occasion, the Prince was rewarded with the Iron Cross. They were married in the presence of the Emperor, Hermine and a few guests. They left the day after the wedding for a church ceremony in Berlin.[186] It would be the last happy occasion at Doorn.

On 1 March 1941, the Emperor suddenly became faint while chopping wood. He took to his bed and it took over two months before he was sufficiently recovered. Hermine then felt safe to undergo a necessary operation herself. On 14 May 1941, she had an operation on her left eye under local anaesthesia. She was still in hospital two weeks later when an alarming report came from Doorn. Even the Emperor's children hurried to Doorn to say goodbye, but the acute danger passed. Only Princess Viktoria Luise, Prince Ludwig Ferdinand, Prince Franz Karl and Henriette stayed behind.

In her memoirs Viktoria Luise wrote, "Then I went into my father's room. He was lying very still. His first question to me was: 'Have you any news of Friederike (Viktoria Luise's daughter)?' Her picture stood next to his bed, for he loved her dearly. He looked at me most imploringly, as if he had waited only for my arrival to tell him something about his fate. But I knew nothing, either, though I could not bring myself to tell him so. Instead, I said: 'Yes, she is well.' He looked as if he had been relieved of a heavy burden and lay back. 'Thank God,' I heard him say. The tension eased from him and he closed his eyes, breathing easily. I sat there motionless while my father slept. The small improvement in his condition was sustained and the doctors there said they through there would be weeks yet before he succumbed. My husband, who had joined me in the meantime with August Wilhelm, went back home, as did the others. Besides, board and lodgings were scarce, and the food supply was very short. Only my nephew Prince Ludwig Ferdinand and I remained, for he was a great consolation to his grandfather. When my father spoke to me again, he discussed world affairs and wanted news of this or that, but his thoughts invariably switched to England. He asked: 'Are we still going to attack England?' Very seriously he added: 'Should that really happen – and should we win – we must immediately stretch out our hand to England and go together. Without England we cannot endure.' His eyes seemed fixed in the far distance and seemed to be asking, what will become of our Germany?"[187]

But then on 3 June, he got worse again and an embolism was detected in his lungs. His nurse told him, "Your Majesty, it is better above. With the Most Supreme Lord it is better for us than on earth." He replied, "I am ready. We will see each other again up there. My end is coming. I am sinking, sinking!"[188] He called for Hermine, "Please fetch my wife, it is time to say goodbye!"[189] and his daughter and managed to thank Hermine for 19 years together before fading into unconsciousness. Hermine and Viktoria Luise stayed by the bed all night, listening to the Emperor's laboured breathing. The Emperor passed away at 12.30 in the afternoon of 4 June 1941 – at the age of 82. He was the same age as his beloved grandmother Queen Victoria when she had died. Hermine had become a widow once more. A member of staff later recalled,"The moment when Princess Hermine came down the stairs to tell us the news, I'll never forget. 'The Emperor has just died. His last words were, 'Lord, have mercy on me, a poor sinner', was all she said to us."[190]

In her memoirs Viktoria Luise wrote, "As I went into my

father's room, I could see that the shadow of death had already begun to lengthen. I sat on his right side and took his dear hand. He opened his eyes, but he could no longer speak. I knew, however, that he had recognised me. Hour after hour I sat by my father's bedside with Princess Hermine and Ludwig Ferdinand. Over the bed hung that wonderful picture of my mother by Lenbach and I knew that my parents would soon be reunited. The night went by. Late next morning the Kaiser, my father, died. It was the 4th of June 1941."[191]

The Emperor did not want a grand funeral and he had added a codicil to his will banning the use of swastika flags. In 1933, he had issued the following order: "Should God decree that I should be recalled from this world at a time when there is still no restoration of the Monarchy in Germany, it is my first resolve that if I should go to my eternal rest while in exile in Doorn, then I am provisionally to be buried in Doorn. My coffin shall be placed at a spot opposite the house where my bust is erected in front of the rhododendrons and where my approved tomb, designed and built by Betzner the architect, will be situated. It will be protected against the weather by a canopy. Flowerbeds of cineraria and salvias shall surround the tomb. The solemnities shall be simple, quiet and dignified. No deputations from Germany, no swastika flags, no wreaths. That will apply if H.M. dies in Doorn. If I die in Potsdam, then my bones shall be laid in the mausoleum of the New Palace in between those of the Empress. Military funeral, no swastika flags, no funeral orations, hymns nor prayers."[192]

A special train was arranged so that members of the family could attend the funeral. Hitler was represented by the Reichs Commissioner for the Netherlands, Arthur Seyss-Inquart and a wreath, with swastikas, was sent. Hitler had probably wished to attend himself but in the words of the Emperor's daughter Viktoria Luise, "He wanted to use this opportunity to walk behind the German Kaiser's coffin in front of whole German people and the world, to show them he is the legitimate successor."[193] The family had not wished to cooperate with Hitler's plans for a state funeral in Potsdam. The Crown Prince led the new widow by the arm during the funeral procession. The funeral was short and with military precision. Crown Princess Cecilie and Hermine both wore heavy black veils. The Emperor was buried near his beloved dogs. The mourners sang "Ich bete an die Macht der Liebe" and "Jesu meine Zuversicht." A final 21-gun salute boomed as the family returned to the house.

Chapter 6

Life after the Emperor

The year after the Emperor's death a mausoleum was built with room for two, so that Hermine could eventually rest beside him. The Emperor had ordered that Hermine be well cared for after his death. Even though Doorn had been her home for the last 19 years, she decided to return to Schloss Saabor and only returned to Doorn in January and June to remember her late husband. One source states that the Crown Prince banned Hermine from Doorn.[1] The Crown Prince had inherited the house, but he never lived in it and during the war years, it was occupied by Sigurd von Ilsemann and his wife. In 1945, the house was expropriated, though the Crown Prince fought this decision. The matter was settled out of court long after the Crown Prince was dead and Doorn now has a museum function.[2] Sigurd von Ilsemann stayed on as administrator of the house until he committed suicide in the gatehouse on 6 June 1952.[3]

On the first anniversary of the Emperor's death and upon the completion of the mausoleum, most of the family gathered together. Hermine wrote, "It was very, very nostalgic, in this fairy-tale park, which he first created, which he loved, in which we had done so much together, talked about, and we returned to the now secluded house, where every step recalls memories of the 19 years spent together."[4] In the early hours of 1943, the Old Palace, where Hermine had her apartments, was almost completely destroyed in a bombing. Hermine was in Berlin for a medical treatment and could only watch as her apartment went up in flames. Her last stay at Doorn would be in January 1944 for what would have been the Emperor's 85th birthday. She stayed in the tower building and brought her own provisions with her, some of which she handed out to Dutch friends and the poor.

She was aware that one of her neighbours in Doorn was hiding a Jewish girl.[5] By then, she had suffered the loss of another son. In August 1943 Prince Hans Georg was killed in action while serving as captain in the Second German Army.[6] She wrote to J.B. Kan, the liaison between the Hohenzollern and the Dutch government, "My beloved eldest son Hans-Georg I have given to the Fatherland, he fell in Russia, an endlessly heavy loss for me, as you can imagine."[7]

Her illusions about Hitler had taken a turn somewhat after witnessing the bombing of Berlin the year before. "What kind of misfortune has that man brought over our people?" she confided to a pastor.[8]

Hermine had returned to her estates in Silesia, where most of the staff was gone as they had been posted to the front. On 28 January 1945, Hermine was ordered to evacuate by the Wehrmacht. Hermine, her daughter Caroline Hermine and their secretary, Ursula Topf, left the castle and headed to Rossla where Hermine's sister Ida lived. Hermine lost all her possessions to the Red Army but arrived safely in Rossla. She found solace with the sons of her daughter Henriette, who were staying with Ida, while Henriette and her husband were in Italy. In Rossla, Hermine received a visit from Ernst August, the husband of her stepdaughter Viktoria Luise, who brought her the news of the coming Russian invasion.

Viktoria Luise wrote in her memoirs, "My husband acquainted our neighbours of what we had heard and went to Rossla, too, where Princess Hermine, my father's second wife was staying. After my father's death she had first returned to her own home in Saabor, Silesia, earlier having fled together with a huge stream of refugees, until she reached her sister Ida's house. However, Princess Hermine refused to believe the reports my husband brought her of the forthcoming Russian incursion, as the Americans were already in occupation of her region which at that time included Halle and Leipzig and stretched to the Elbe.

My husband told her: 'You must not stay here, for it's all been decided. You must get away.' She answered: 'The Russians will not come. It won't happen. In any case, the Americans would tell us if there were to be any changes.' My husband continued to urge her to leave. 'You must consider who you are.' He told her, 'You dare not fall into Russian hands.' She replied simply: 'I have nothing to reproach myself for. I'm staying here.'"[9]

On 12 April 1945, Rossla was invaded by the Americans and slowly but surely the true horrors of the war came to light. Hermine was shocked, "With the nameless misery that has come over our poor Germany, there is only one plus to the horror without end, the Nazis are no more."[10]

As the war came to an end, Hermine's stepson the Crown Prince immediately tried to distance himself from the Nazi regime. After his capture by French troops in May 1945, he said, "The German people have behaved like idiots. First, they followed Ebert, then Hindenburg, then Hitler. This war has been madness... I saw Hitler two or three times and each time I told him he was making a mistake. I especially warned him about persecuting Catholics and Jews, but Hitler really hated the Jews."[11] The SS-General Karl Wolff testified after the war, "The only one truly active in the part was Prince August Wilhelm, called Auwi. One had naturally made inroads in these circles, in order to use them as advertisements and publicity for the NSDAP. One frequently invited them to large assemblies and rallies and gave them an appropriate place where they could be seen by all."[12]

In April 1945, Hermine was interviewed by two reporters at Rossla and a German-born Jewish soldier serving with the United States Army named Rudolph Daniel Sichel who wrote to his parents about her. On 28 April 1945, he reported home.

"Dear folks,
At last I have found some time to write you and answer your

letters. We were really quite busy but now we are resting and waiting for the end of the war. At least that is what it looks like at the moment... how they can still hold out is beyond me.

Now to your letter no. 107 which arrived a few days ago. I really was very interested to see all these clippings with my name in it – I am also gald (sic) that by this manner you received speedy news of my well being (sic). Well it looks really noce (sic) to see my name in print. I remeher (sic) that interview very well and frankly I was not all impressed by the Kaiserin. Nobility especailly (sic) in Germany does not impress me. I was helping out these two reporters doing their interview. First, we interviewed the House Manager whi (sic) was a typical example of a German who changed his colors lately. (One of a million)

At the end of the conversation the reporters requested the manager that they would like to speak to the Empress. The manager replied, (it was around noon time) I am sorry, but the Empress is sleeping and cannot be disturbed. That's when I made the famous statement. Tell her, there is a War going on and we the Americans want to see her. Go and get her.

Afetr (sic) a few minutes he returned and said the Empress was ready to see him x them. I intentionally did not go with them. First of all, she speaks very good English and secondly, I already had talked to her before. Besides she is not a young girl and I was sick and tired of listening to that shit."[13]

The interview appeared in the Daily News on 17 April 1945:

"The gray-haired old lady sat upright in her chair, fingering the long strand of pearls around her neck. 'Technically,' she said, 'we are still enemies: We are German; you are American.' She paused a moment. This was the Empress Hermine, the widow of the Kaiser of Germany. With a half-dozen other Hohenzollerns and former royalty, she is now in American hands. The Empress gazed at a photograph on the table – a photograph of Wilhelm II, taken three weeks before his death at Doorn. 'I loved him,' she said. 'He was a poor old man with the wrong sort of children, but I loved him. He loved Germany and I love Germany. We wanted to make a real Germany. By the way, do you have any of the latest American books on politics? Do you by chance have any real coffee?'

The empress has been in American custody for two days, and since the American came her 84-room castle, where she is living with six other royal personages, has been used as a temporary Army command post. Those with her are the Princess Ida, her sister; the Princess Carmo Hartung, her niece; Prince Christoph Martin, the Countess Therese of Stolberg and her children, Prince Franz Josef of Prussia, 2, and Prince Fritz, 6 months old. Two months ago, Hermine came here from a castle in Silesia. The royal party fled only an hour before the Russians arrived. When I walked into the spacious grounds where the castle stands, the director of the estate said Hermine was asleep and was not to be disturbed.

Sergt. Rudolf Chicle (sic), New York City, said: 'Wake her up!' The director went off in a hurry. Lieut. Harry Doyle, 68th St. Brooklyn, came up and said: 'Treat this babe nice. She's a friend of mine.' We told her the war was finished, to all practical purposes and that Germany again had been defeated. A few tears glistened on her cheeks. She was silent a moment and said: 'I love Germany.'"[14]

When the Americans left on 2 July, they were replaced by the Red Army. Hermine was ordered to report to the Torgau camp, but she was soon picked up by two men, one in a Russian uniform, and was asked to come to Berlin. Her secretary tried to talk her out of going but Hermine packed a suitcase with clothes for two days. Eventually, she was taken to a residential area on the outskirts of Frankfurt an der Oder, the Paulinenhof. She was taken to a villa that had been abandoned by the owners as they fled from the Red Army. She was lodged on the upper floor while the lower floor was for her guards. "She was the only one (of the family) to be caught in the East, but both Auwi (Prince August Wilhelm) and the Crown Prince (Wilhelm) died, their spirits broken by their experiences of internment."[15]

An interpreter brought one hot meal a day from the nearby military hospital for Hermine, which she was grateful for. Hermine was allowed to take walks and returned to the habit she once formed with her husband. One of the guards took pity on Hermine and gave her his gloves. She was allowed to have a radio and she was allowed to buy newspapers, which were her only connections to the outside world. Hermine and her secretary were reunited on Christmas Day 1945 when her secretary was allowed to bring by her youngest grandson, Franz Friedrich, who had been born in 1944. The following year, the empty house was finally furnished with some borrowed furniture and internment became a bit more bearable. Hermine set up a living room where she also ate and a small bedroom. The third room was for her secretary and Franz Friedrich. Despite being interned, she was able to move around in the city and she was allowed to receive visitors. She did not receive any answers on whether she would ever be released but she was treated courteously and even received the highest possible food card.

In early 1946, a British journalist, who had learned of Hermine's internment, wrote to the British Foreign Minister Bevin and King George VI. The response was "It is not thought desirable for His Majesty's Government to take any action in this matter" and "any suggestion that we were hobnobbing with the German royal family would be eagerly seized on by the Russians or anyone else who likes to call us revolutionary."[16]

In July 1946, she was suddenly no longer allowed to walk alone, and all visitors had to report to the guards first. Her guards could make her life easier or they could make it a hell. She was not allowed to react to harassment, and she felt robbed of her freedom. She now only lived for her young grandson. She arranged for his baptism to take place in her living room, a few days after his first birthday.

On 14 April 1947, several American journalists were allowed to enter the Paulinenhof and interview Hermine. The Red Army wanted to show the world that she was in good health, but Hermine was barely able to fit so many people in her living room. She asked the press not to write bad things about her and the interview appeared in the New York Herald Tribune. Just two months before the interview Hermine was robbed of her fur coat and handbag.[17] A Dutch newspaper reported on the interview, "The widow of the former Emperor Wilhelm II known as Empress Hermine has been interviewed by some American reporters. She lives in an apartment with six rooms, which she shares with seven other people, including her two-and-half-year-old grandson Franz Friedrich of Prussia, a secretary, a driver and his family, and a Russian who acts as a nanny and a translator. During the interview she sat on a chaise-longue. She stroked her grandson. The walls of the room were filled with portraits of the deceased former Emperor. The interview took place in the presence of four Russian officers. Among them was the commander of the town, Colonel Jacob Keshikov. Princess Hermine said that the Russians would not allow her to leave the city. She answered several questions with the remark, 'Don't bother me with that now.' Princess Hermine who married the Emperor in 1922 lived with him in Doorn until he died in June 1941. In August 1941, she left Doorn to live on an estate in Silesia. At the end of the war she was taken to Frankfurt on the Oder. While being bombarded with questions about the Emperor, Hermine said, 'The Emperor distrusted Hitler from the beginning. The Emperor was afraid for Germany and the world and despised Hitler.' She said that they were basically prisoners when the Germans invaded the Netherlands. 'We suffered a lot because the SS had received the order from Hitler to guard us.' Hermine told them that the Emperor did not say, 'The only way I would want to go to England is with victorious German troops.' While Hermine spoke, her German secretary privately said, 'The Empress is literally a prisoner here and cannot make a move without permission from the Russians.' Hermine said that she was still corresponding with friends in the United States. Among them was the painter Emil Alborn who lived in Boston. She wanted a provisions package from friends in the United States."[18]

Another report of the interview adds that Hermine answered, "We do not receive what we are used to," when she was asked if she received enough food. Of the Russian nanny she said, "She accompanies me when I take walks. I don't know her name. She says she is called Miss Nina."[19]

Hermine always remained ready for a chance to escape, she even had a well-hidden suitcase full of money and jewels. However, shortly after she had given the suitcase to her son, it was stolen from him, effectively ending her chances of ever escaping.[20] Those jewels would cause quite the scandal yet.

On 5 August, Hermine began to feel tired at a tea party. A doctor diagnosed purulent tonsillitis and an abscess formed, which the doctor wanted to cut open to help Hermine breathe. However, he did not consider it necessary that she was hospitalised. By 7 August, Hermine's neck was so swollen that she was no longer able to eat and drink. Breathing suddenly became very hard and when the doctor finally arrived, there was very little he could do. She died later that same day of a heart attack as she was supported by Ursula.

Shortly after her death, her last interview was published.

"Describing her life in the Russian Zone as little different from life at Doorn, the ex-Kaiser's widow, Princess Hermine von Schoenaich-Carolath said just before she died a few days ago: 'In Holland I was forever watched by the Gestapo. Here it is the Russian secret police.' The interview was her last, as it was also her last contact with the Western world. She looked wan and worn and nearer seventy than her real age of less than sixty years. With queenly dignity, she said: 'There is one thing I should like the world to know. It is not true that I went into hiding at the fall of Berlin, nor was I discovered by the Russian living on the Hohenzollern estates near the Oder disguised as a peasant woman. That was an invention put out by the Russians to discredit monarchy for their own purposes. I was never crowned a German empress, but they call me majesty, as do many of my own people. The truth is that the Russians brought me from Potsdam to Frankfort themselves. I was living in Potsdam and I was there the night, near the end of the war, when it was bombed by the British. I have heard that that was a special bombing – to symbolize the end of Prussian militarism. But all I remember was the horror and terror of that fearful night, and the destruction we saw in the morning. The beautiful buildings of the town were ruined. Then came the battle of Berlin, and still I stayed on in Potsdam. Thus, I was there when the first Red Army men came into the town and conquered the ruins. The Russians took me prisoner, and I was under guard at the time of the Potsdam conference, though I had no desire to interfere in politics. Later on, inquiries were made about me by members of the Hohenzollern family, and my own family through diplomatic channels. I did not know this but one day I found myself taken to Frankfort-on-Oder. Some Hohenzollern estates are nearby, but they have all been expropriated and split up into small parcels. Here I was released under close surveillance with the warning that if I said anything indiscreet I should find myself back in close confinement again. Now, please, do not publish this abroad till after my death. That may not be long now – I seem to get weaker all the time, despite the fact that my all household have No 1 rations available in the Russian zone. I have been allowed to see some visitors, including the press and some survivors of the Kaiser's court at Doorn,' she added, 'but they have all come with a Russian escort and I have been to talk only in their presence.'

Two Russian girl students were assigned to live with Hermine as agents of the Soviet secret police. One she described as her 'official Russian interpreter and guardian.' But she gave her last interview in circumstances that, for the present, can not be revealed. At that interview no Russians were present, and she spoke thus with immensely greater freedom than she did when interviewed by the American correspondents who saw her during last April's conducted tour of Red Germany.

Hermine was the daughter of Prince Henry XXII of Reuss. She first married Prince John George of Schoenaich-Carolath. She married the ex-Kaiser in 1922. In Frankfort, her home was a three-room apartment where she lived with her three-year-old grandson, Franz Friedrich, prince of Prussia. The child's fate is not known. His father was killed in the war. The boy was reported very much upset by his grandmother's death. He had been promised a big celebration for her sixtieth birthday on Dec. 17. "It is not hard to remember," Princess Hermine is quoted as having told him. "It is four days before Stalin's!"[21]

Her missing jewels were now suddenly a source of fascination. Her son Prince Ferdinand Johann and his wife even took a truth serum to satisfy the curiosity of the investigators. He claimed that the jewels had disappeared from a trunk in the house of an American friend. The Prince told investigators that he was certain that "he had been betrayed to the Russians while playing a cat and mouse game with them and moving from apartment to apartment in an effort to shake them off."[22] He also said that the 96 pieces, including gem-studded tiaras, earrings, brooches, combs, toilet sets, snuff and power boxes, bracelets, rings and watches were worth 50,000,000 marks or $5,000,000 at the time. Of those 96 pieces, 29 had been stolen and those were valued at

$2,000,000. The truth serum reportedly knocked him out for six hours. "Troubles never come singly. Now Mama is dead, and I cannot even go to the funeral because I am sure the Russians would arrest me because I am anti-Communist."[23]

Then came the rumours that Hermine must have been poisoned by the thieves who also stole the jewels. An American army spokesman said, "Heart failure can be caused by many things, including poison or drugs." They were also going to question Vera Herbst, one of the guests at the tea party and reportedly the mistress of Prince Ferdinand Johann.[24] On 12 August, Prince Ferdinand Johann told *Die Welt*, "I have no grounds to assume that my mother, the widow of Emperor Wilhelm II, died an unnatural death."[25] Vera Herbst was arrested on charges of murder and theft but was released the following day as investigators admitted they had wanted to scare her. The case was then turned over to the German police.[26] Vera had reportedly smuggled several of Hermine's jewels out of the Soviet zone and it is not entirely clear if the 29 missing pieces were ever recovered.

Hermine's last will and testament however was clear. She wanted to return to Doorn to be buried next to the Emperor; the mausoleum there had been built for two. The Russians agreed to let Hermine's body go to the Netherlands shortly after her death in 1947, but the Doorn municipality refused to cooperate after the news leaked in the press. The final decision was made by the Allied Control Council upon the suggestion of Crown Prince Wilhelm and Hermine was interred in the Antique Temple in Sansoucci Park in Potsdam, where the Emperor's first wife was also buried. On 15 August 1947, Hermine made her last journey from her internment to her place of rest. Outside the villa, the people of Frankfurt an der Oder laid an abundance of flowers and wreaths. Her body was taken by lorry to Potsdam in coffin decorated with purple brocade[27] and only her eldest daughter made it to Potsdam. Her young grandson was also there, in the arms of her secretary. The Antique Temple had been ransacked during the chaotic days in 1945 and only Auguste Viktoria's tomb had remained untouched, presumably because they had been unable to move heavy marble plate. The other remains had been thrown about and dishonoured.[28] Hermine's body was transferred on an old lorry with six regular cars following behind, one of which had a flat on its way to Potsdam. The coffin was lifted from the lorry without ceremony and carried into the Antique Temple. There were several reporters outside the temple. A vicar named Willigmann from Berlin recited John 14:27, *Peace I leave with you, my peace I give to you.* Though the service was kept short, also due to the intense heat, an older lady was forced to sit down on the steps of the temple.[29]

Her mourning card made by Prince Ferdinand Johann read, "God, whose ways we so often do not understand in our time, took my beloved mother EMPRESS DOWAGER HERMINE OF PRUSSIA on 7 August 1947 at 12.25 o'clock to him. A sudden heart attack released her from uncertainty and deep emotional suffering. Her heart's desire, to see her beloved Fatherland again and to be with her children, was not fulfilled. Her life, the fulfilment of her high duty, loyalty and love, ended much too soon. Until the transfer of my mother to the Mausoleum in Doorn (Holland), the internment will take place on Friday 15 August 1947 at 2 o'clock in the Antique Temple in Potsdam."[30]

Just as the case for the missing jewels was underway, Ferdinand Johann was arrested for concealing his membership to the Nazi party to get a job as a British army chauffeur. He was arrested just mere hours after Hermine's funeral. He would eventually win his appeal after the court found that it was not proven "beyond doubt that he had knowingly made a false statement" on his questionnaire.[31] In September newspapers reported on Hermine's will, "Princess Hermine, who died last month at Frankfurt on the Oder, left a will stipulating that her $500,000 jewel fortune, now held in safekeeping by the United

States Army, be divided among Prince Ferdinand von Schönaich-Carolath and his sisters, the Princesses Hermine Caroline and Henrietta. Reports that the Hohenzollerns had asked for a portion of the fortune brought this comment today from Prince Ferdinand: 'To my knowledge the Hohenzollerns have asked only for the return of medals of the former Kaiser which were left with my mother when he died.' The Hohenzollern clan is headed by Prince Friedrich Wilhelm. Prince Ferdinand said now that the will had been filed for probate, he would ask Gen. Lucius D. Clay, United States Military Governor, for early release of the jewels held in trusteeships by the United States authorities. Another portion of the royal jewels, also valued at about $500,000 or more, was reported by Prince Ferdinand to have been stolen from him two months ago."[32]

In May 1948, Prince Ferdinand, Henriette and Caroline Hermine tried to obtain permission to have their mother transferred to Doorn. They wrote to the Dutch Military Mission in Berlin, "The undersigned, the biological children of Empress Dowager Hermine of Prussia, who died on 7 August 1947 in Frankfurt / Oder, again ask for permission to transfer the sarcophagus of her Majesty Empress Dowager Hermine. It was her last will to find her last resting place in Doorn, where she had lived for 19 years and found a home by the side of His Majesty Emperor Wilhelm II in the Doorner Mausoleum. Since the Dutch government had already given the permission for the transfer in August of last year, for which the undersigned were grateful, if the necessary formalities could now also be followed, so that the transfer in fulfilment of the last wish of the deceased can take place."[33]

Once again everything was agreed upon and it appears that even the Doorn municipality was in agreement this time. The Minister of Foreign Affairs agreed to let her children come over but in November 1948, Hermine's secretary Ursula Topf wrote, "Unfortunately, referring to the various talks and your letter of 3

September, I have to inform you today that the difficulties which have arisen due to the blockade of Berlin have become so great that it has become impossible to transfer the sarcophagus of Empress Hermine at this time. If the conditions for the transfer can be established in the foreseeable future, you can contact me again and ask for their early support in the completion of the formalities."[34] Hermine's wish has remained unfulfilled until now.

Hermine was a complicated woman who lived during a complicated time. Her second marriage to the exiled Emperor had given her ambitions that led to her involvement with the Nazis and to a hope of restoration. Despite this, she was also heavily involved in charitable works and cared very much for her children, who were her main concern when she made the decision to marry again. Her role in history has been largely forgotten and she has been overshadowed by her predecessor Auguste Viktoria and her larger than life husband, the Kaiser.

Notes

Introduction

1. Scheel, Klaus, *1933 – Der Tag von Potsdam,* Brandenburghisches Verlagshaus, Berlin, 1996 p.71-72

2. Empress Hermine, *Days in Doorn,* Hutchinson, London, 1928 p. 159

Chapter 1

1. Empress Hermine, *Days in Doorn,* Hutchinson, London, 1928 p.39

2. Reuss, Hermine, *Mijn leven en hoe ik den keizer trouwde,* Weekblad Het Leven, Amsterdam, ca. 1930 p.6

3. Empress Hermine, *Days in Doorn,* Hutchinson, London, 1928 p.38

4. Empress Hermine, *Days in Doorn,* Hutchinson, London, 1928 p.44

5. This is probably a mix-up of two of Princess Ida's aunts. Mathilde of Schaumburg-Lippe was married to Duke Eugen of Württemberg and Adelheid of Schaumburg-Lippe was married to Friedrich, Duke of Schleswig-Holstein-Sonderburg-Glücksburg. Both were widowed in 1888 and it is unclear which of the aunts acted as godmother.

6. Toom, den, Friedhild & Klein, Sven Michael, Hermine – *Die zweite Gemahlin von Wilhelm II,* Verein für Greizer Geschichte, Greiz, 2007 p.10-11

7. Empress Hermine, *Days in Doorn,* Hutchinson, London, 1928 p.53

8. Empress Hermine, *Days in Doorn,* Hutchinson, London, 1928 p.53

9. Toom, den, Friedhild & Klein, Sven Michael, Hermine – *Die zweite Gemahlin von Wilhelm II,* Verein für Greizer Geschichte, Greiz, 2007 p.16

10. Empress Hermine, *Days in Doorn*, Hutchinson, London, 1928 p.62
11. Toom, den, Friedhild & Klein, Sven Michael, Hermine – *Die zweite Gemahlin von Wilhelm II*, Verein für Greizer Geschichte, Greiz, 2007 p.17
12. Toom, den, Friedhild & Klein, Sven Michael, Hermine – *Die zweite Gemahlin von Wilhelm II*, Verein für Greizer Geschichte, Greiz, 2007 p.16
13. Toom, den, Friedhild & Klein, Sven Michael, Hermine – *Die zweite Gemahlin von Wilhelm II*, Verein für Greizer Geschichte, Greiz, 2007 p.18-19
14. Toom, den, Friedhild & Klein, Sven Michael, Hermine – *Die zweite Gemahlin von Wilhelm II*, Verein für Greizer Geschichte, Greiz, 2007 p.19
15. Empress Hermine, *Days in Doorn*, Hutchinson, London, 1928 p.66
16. Empress Hermine, *Days in Doorn*, Hutchinson, London, 1928 p.70
17. *Ibid.*
18. Empress Hermine, *Days in Doorn*, Hutchinson, London, 1928 p.71
19. Empress Hermine, *Days in Doorn*, Hutchinson, London, 1928 p.71-72
20. Empress Hermine, *Days in Doorn*, Hutchinson, London, 1928 p.42
21. Empress Hermine, *Days in Doorn*, Hutchinson, London, 1928 p.43
22. Toom, den, Friedhild & Klein, Sven Michael, Hermine – *Die zweite Gemahlin von Wilhelm II*, Verein für Greizer Geschichte, Greiz, 2007 p.20
23. Toom, den, Friedhild & Klein, Sven Michael, Hermine – *Die zweite Gemahlin von Wilhelm II*, Verein für Greizer Geschichte, Greiz, 2007 p.22
24. Empress Hermine, *Days in Doorn*, Hutchinson, London,

1928 p.73

25. Empress Hermine, *Days in Doorn*, Hutchinson, London, 1928 p.74

26. Empress Hermine, *Days in Doorn*, Hutchinson, London, 1928 p.75

27. Toom, den, Friedhild & Klein, Sven Michael, Hermine – Die zweite Gemahlin von Wilhelm II, Verein für Greizer Geschichte, Greiz, 2007 p.24

28. Empress Hermine, *Days in Doorn*, Hutchinson, London, 1928 p.77

29. Empress Hermine, *Days in Doorn*, Hutchinson, London, 1928 p.78

30. Reibnitz, von, Kurt, *Wilhelm ll. Und Hermine, Geschichte und Kritik von Doorn*, Reissner, Dresden, 1929 p.64

31. Empress Hermine, *Days in Doorn*, Hutchinson, London, 1928 p.79

32. Empress Hermine, *Days in Doorn*, Hutchinson, London, 1928 p.87

33. Empress Hermine, *Days in Doorn*, Hutchinson, London, 1928 p.84

34. Reibnitz, von, Kurt, *Wilhelm ll. Und Hermine, Geschichte und Kritik von Doorn*, Reissner, Dresden, 1929 p.66

35. Empress Hermine, *Days in Doorn*, Hutchinson, London, 1928 p.89

36. Reibnitz, von, Kurt, *Wilhelm ll. Und Hermine, Geschichte und Kritik von Doorn*, Reissner, Dresden, 1929 p.68

37. *Ibid.*

38. Toom, den, Friedhild & Klein, Sven Michael, Hermine – *Die zweite Gemahlin von Wilhelm II*, Verein für Greizer Geschichte, Greiz, 2007 p.27

39. Toom, den, Friedhild & Klein, Sven Michael, Hermine – *Die zweite Gemahlin von Wilhelm II*, Verein für Greizer Geschichte, Greiz, 2007 p.28

40. Reibnitz, von, Kurt, *Wilhelm ll. Und Hermine, Geschichte und*

Kritik von Doorn, Reissner, Dresden, 1929 p.69

41. Empress Hermine, *Days in Doorn*, Hutchinson, London, 1928 p.91
42. Empress Hermine, *Days in Doorn*, Hutchinson, London, 1928 p.94
43. Reibnitz, von, Kurt, *Wilhelm ll. Und Hermine, Geschichte und Kritik von Doorn*, Reissner, Dresden, 1929 p.70

Chapter 2

1. Toom, den, Friedhild & Klein, Sven Michael, Hermine – *Die zweite Gemahlin von Wilhelm II*, Verein für Greizer Geschichte, Greiz, 2007 p.33-36
2. Reuss, Hermine, *Mijn leven en hoe ik den keizer trouwde*, Weekblad Het Leven, Amsterdam, ca. 1930 p.26
3. Empress Hermine, *Days in Doorn*, Hutchinson, London, 1928 p.98
4. Toom, den, Friedhild & Klein, Sven Michael, Hermine – *Die zweite Gemahlin von Wilhelm II*, Verein für Greizer Geschichte, Greiz, 2007 p.37
5. Empress Hermine, *Days in Doorn*, Hutchinson, London, 1928 p.105
6. Empress Hermine, *Days in Doorn*, Hutchinson, London, 1928 p.105-106
7. Empress Hermine, *Days in Doorn*, Hutchinson, London, 1928 p.99
8. Reuss, Hermine, *Mijn leven en hoe ik den keizer trouwde*, Weekblad Het Leven, Amsterdam, ca. 1930 p.42
9. Empress Hermine, *Days in Doorn*, Hutchinson, London, 1928 p.127
10. Empress Hermine, *Days in Doorn*, Hutchinson, London, 1928 p.132
11. Empress Hermine, *Days in Doorn*, Hutchinson, London, 1928 p.133
12. Reibnitz, von, Kurt, *Wilhelm ll. Und Hermine, Geschichte und*

Kritik von Doorn, Reissner, Dresden, 1929 p.96

13. Empress Hermine, *Days in Doorn*, Hutchinson, London, 1928 p.155
14. Empress Hermine, *Days in Doorn*, Hutchinson, London, 1928 p.159

Chapter 3

1. MacDonogh, Giles, *The Last Kaiser – The Life of Wilhelm II*, St. Martin's Press, New York, 2000 p.21-22
2. Fulford, Roger (edited), *Dearest Child – Letters between Queen Victoria and the Princess Royal*, Holt, Rinehart and Winston, New York, 1964 p.159
3. Fulford, Roger (edited), *Dearest Child – Letters between Queen Victoria and the Princess Royal*, Holt, Rinehart and Winston, New York, 1964 p.164
4. MacDonogh, Giles, *The Last Kaiser – The Life of Wilhelm II*, St. Martin's Press, New York, 2000 p.23
5. MacDonogh, Giles, *The Last Kaiser – The Life of Wilhelm II*, St. Martin's Press, New York, 2000 p.37-38
6. MacDonogh, Giles, *The Last Kaiser – The Life of Wilhelm II*, St. Martin's Press, New York, 2000 p.43
7. MacDonogh, Giles, *The Last Kaiser – The Life of Wilhelm II*, St. Martin's Press, New York, 2000 p.49
8. MacDonogh, Giles, *The Last Kaiser – The Life of Wilhelm II*, St. Martin's Press, New York, 2000 p.51
9. MacDonogh, Giles, *The Last Kaiser – The Life of Wilhelm II*, St. Martin's Press, New York, 2000 p.55
10. She later became the wife of Tsar Nicholas II of Russia.
11. Kiste, van der, John, *The last German Empress*, CreateSpace Independent Publishing Platform, Scotts Valley, 2015 p.10-11
12. Kiste, van der, John, *The last German Empress*, CreateSpace Independent Publishing Platform, Scotts Valley, 2015 p.11
13. MacDonogh, Giles, *The Last Kaiser – The Life of Wilhelm II*, St.

Martin's Press, New York, 2000 p.61

14. Kiste, van der, John, *The last German Empress*, CreateSpace Independent Publishing Platform, Scotts Valley, 2015 p.17

15. Kiste, van der, John, *The last German Empress*, CreateSpace Independent Publishing Platform, Scotts Valley, 2015 p.18

16. MacDonogh, Giles, *The Last Kaiser – The Life of Wilhelm II*, St. Martin's Press, New York, 2000 p.69

17. Kiste, van der, John, *The last German Empress*, CreateSpace Independent Publishing Platform, Scotts Valley, 2015 p.21

18. MacDonogh, Giles, *The Last Kaiser – The Life of Wilhelm II*, St. Martin's Press, New York, 2000 p.91

19. MacDonogh, Giles, *The Last Kaiser – The Life of Wilhelm II*, St. Martin's Press, New York, 2000 p.104

20. Kiste, van der, John, *The last German Empress*, CreateSpace Independent Publishing Platform, Scotts Valley, 2015 p.29

21. Ramm, Agatha (edited), *Beloved & darling child : last letters between Queen Victoria and her eldest daughter, 1886-1901*, Sutton Publishing, Stroud, 1998 p. 72-73

22. MacDonogh, Giles, *The Last Kaiser – The Life of Wilhelm II*, St. Martin's Press, New York, 2000 p.130

23. MacDonogh, Giles, *The Last Kaiser – The Life of Wilhelm II*, St. Martin's Press, New York, 2000 p.131

24. Kiste, van der, John, *The last German Empress*, CreateSpace Independent Publishing Platform, Scotts Valley, 2015 p.50

25. Richards, Stewart, *Curtain down at Her Majesty's*, The History Press, Stroud, 2019 p. 47-48

26. MacDonogh, Giles, *The Last Kaiser – The Life of Wilhelm II*, St. Martin's Press, New York, 2000 p.264

27. Kiste, van der, John, *The last German Empress*, CreateSpace Independent Publishing Platform, Scotts Valley, 2015 p.60

28. Kiste, van der, John, *The last German Empress*, CreateSpace Independent Publishing Platform, Scotts Valley, 2015 p.62

29. Kiste, van der, John, *The last German Empress*, CreateSpace Independent Publishing Platform, Scotts Valley, 2015 p.64

30. Kiste, van der, John, *The last German Empress*, CreateSpace Independent Publishing Platform, Scotts Valley, 2015 p.65

31. Kiste, van der, John, *The last German Empress*, CreateSpace Independent Publishing Platform, Scotts Valley, 2015 p.67

32. Kiste, van der, John, *The last German Empress*, CreateSpace Independent Publishing Platform, Scotts Valley, 2015 p.74

33. Kiste, van der, John, *The last German Empress*, CreateSpace Independent Publishing Platform, Scotts Valley, 2015 p.75-76

34. MacDonogh, Giles, *The Last Kaiser – The Life of Wilhelm II*, St. Martin's Press, New York, 2000 p.360

35. Kiste, van der, John, *The last German Empress*, CreateSpace Independent Publishing Platform, Scotts Valley, 2015 p.79

36. Kiste, van der, John, *The last German Empress*, CreateSpace Independent Publishing Platform, Scotts Valley, 2015 p.80-82

37. Kiste, van der, John, *The last German Empress*, CreateSpace Independent Publishing Platform, Scotts Valley, 2015 p.83

38. Kiste, van der, John, *The last German Empress*, CreateSpace Independent Publishing Platform, Scotts Valley, 2015 p.86

39. Kiste, van der, John, *The last German Empress*, CreateSpace Independent Publishing Platform, Scotts Valley, 2015 p.86-87

40. Kiste, van der, John, *The last German Empress*, CreateSpace Independent Publishing Platform, Scotts Valley, 2015 p.88

41. MacDonogh, Giles, *The Last Kaiser – The Life of Wilhelm II*, St. Martin's Press, New York, 2000 p.413

42. Fasseur, Cees, *Wilhelmina – De jonge koningin*, Uitgeverij Balans, Amsterdam, 1998 p.552

43. Graaf, de, Beatrice, *Vorstin op vredespad*, Tijdschrift voor Geschiedenis v131 n4, 2018, p.591

44. Fasseur, Cees, *Wilhelmina – De jonge koningin*, Uitgeverij Balans, Amsterdam, 1998 p.554

45. Moeyes, Paul, *Het kleine keizersdrama in Amerongen*, Stichting

Kasteel Amerongen, Amerongen, 2018 p.63

46. Moeyes, Paul, *Het kleine keizersdrama in Amerongen*, Stichting Kasteel Amerongen, Amerongen, 2018 p.65

47. Koninklijk Huisarchief A50 – *Telegram 11 November 1918*

48. Kiste, van der, John, *The last German Empress*, CreateSpace Independent Publishing Platform, Scotts Valley, 2015 p.89-90

49. Moeyes, Paul, *Het kleine keizersdrama in Amerongen*, Stichting Kasteel Amerongen, Amerongen, 2018 p.70

50. Mansel, Philip and Riotte, Torsten, *Monarchy and exile: The politics of legitimacy from Marie de Médicis to Wilhelm II*, Palgrave Macmillan, Basingstoke, 2011 p.339

51. Kiste, van der, John, *The last German Empress*, CreateSpace Independent Publishing Platform, Scotts Valley, 2015 p.94

52. Kiste, van der, John, *The last German Empress*, CreateSpace Independent Publishing Platform, Scotts Valley, 2015 p.95

53. MacDonogh, Giles, *The Last Kaiser – The Life of Wilhelm II*, St. Martin's Press, New York, 2000 p.423

54. Moeyes, Paul, *Het kleine keizersdrama in Amerongen*, Stichting Kasteel Amerongen, Amerongen, 2018 p.81

55. Moeyes, Paul, *Het kleine keizersdrama in Amerongen*, Stichting Kasteel Amerongen, Amerongen, 2018 p.111

56. Moeyes, Paul, *Het kleine keizersdrama in Amerongen*, Stichting Kasteel Amerongen, Amerongen, 2018 p.113

57. Moeyes, Paul, *Het kleine keizersdrama in Amerongen*, Stichting Kasteel Amerongen, Amerongen, 2018 p.115

58. Mansel, Philip and Riotte, Torsten, *Monarchy and exile: The politics of legitimacy from Marie de Médicis to Wilhelm II*, Palgrave Macmillan, Basingstoke, 2011 p.339

59. Kiste, van der, John, *The last German Empress*, CreateSpace Independent Publishing Platform, Scotts Valley, 2015 p.97

60. Kiste, van der, John, *The last German Empress*, CreateSpace Independent Publishing Platform, Scotts Valley, 2015 p.100

61. Kiste, van der, John, *The last German Empress*, CreateSpace

Independent Publishing Platform, Scotts Valley, 2015 p.104-105

62. Kiste, van der, John, *The last German Empress*, CreateSpace Independent Publishing Platform, Scotts Valley, 2015 p.106

63. *Ibid.*

64. Kiste, van der, John, *The last German Empress*, CreateSpace Independent Publishing Platform, Scotts Valley, 2015 p.107

65. Mansel, Philip and Riotte, Torsten, *Monarchy and exile: The politics of legitimacy from Marie de Médicis to Wilhelm II*, Palgrave Macmillan, Basingstoke, 2011 p.340

Chapter 4

1. Empress Hermine, *Days in Doorn*, Hutchinson, London, 1928 p.189

2. Reuss, Hermine, *Mijn leven en hoe ik den keizer trouwde*, Weekblad Het Leven, Amsterdam, ca. 1930 p.63

3. Empress Hermine, *Days in Doorn*, Hutchinson, London, 1928 p. XX-XXI

4. Reuss, Hermine, *Mijn leven en hoe ik den keizer trouwde*, Weekblad Het Leven, Amsterdam, ca. 1930 p.64

5. Reuss, Hermine, *Mijn leven en hoe ik den keizer trouwde*, Weekblad Het Leven, Amsterdam, ca. 1930 p.65

6. Empress Hermine, *Days in Doorn*, Hutchinson, London, 1928 p. XXI-XXII

7. Empress Hermine, *Days in Doorn*, Hutchinson, London, 1928 p.196-197

8. Reuss, Hermine, *Mijn leven en hoe ik den keizer trouwde*, Weekblad Het Leven, Amsterdam, ca. 1930 p.66-67

9. Reuss, Hermine, *Mijn leven en hoe ik den keizer trouwde*, Weekblad Het Leven, Amsterdam, ca. 1930 p.68

10. Reuss, Hermine, *Mijn leven en hoe ik den keizer trouwde*, Weekblad Het Leven, Amsterdam, ca. 1930 p.69

11. *Ibid.*

12. Empress Hermine, *Days in Doorn*, Hutchinson, London,

1928 p.184

13. Reuss, Hermine, *Mijn leven en hoe ik den keizer trouwde*, Weekblad Het Leven, Amsterdam, ca. 1930 p.72

14. Reuss, Hermine, *Mijn leven en hoe ik den keizer trouwde*, Weekblad Het Leven, Amsterdam, ca. 1930 p.74-75

15. Empress Hermine, *Days in Doorn*, Hutchinson, London, 1928 p.205-206

16. Empress Hermine, *Days in Doorn*, Hutchinson, London, 1928 p.77-78

17. Röhl, John C.G., *Wilhelm II – Into the Abyss of War and Exile 1900-1941*, Cambridge University Press, Cambridge, 2015 p.1209

18. Empress Hermine, *Days in Doorn*, Hutchinson, London, 1928 p.107

19. Empress Hermine, *Days in Doorn*, Hutchinson, London, 1928 p.108-109

20. Bataviaasch nieuwsblad (09-12-1922) Een Interview met Prinses Hermine

21. Toom, den, Friedhild & Klein, Sven Michael, Hermine – *Die zweite Gemahlin von Wilhelm II*, Verein für Greizer Geschichte, Greiz, 2007 p.50

22. *Ibid.*

23. Toom, den, Friedhild & Klein, Sven Michael, Hermine – *Die zweite Gemahlin von Wilhelm II*, Verein für Greizer Geschichte, Greiz, 2007 p.51

24. Toom, den, Friedhild & Klein, Sven Michael, Hermine – *Die zweite Gemahlin von Wilhelm II*, Verein für Greizer Geschichte, Greiz, 2007 p.52

25. Ilsemann, von, Sigurd, *Wilhelm II in Nederland 1918 – 1941*, Uitgeverij Aspekt, Soesterberg, 2015 p.188

26. Ilsemann, von, Sigurd, *Wilhelm II in Nederland 1918 – 1941*, Uitgeverij Aspekt, Soesterberg, 2015 p.173

27. MacDonogh, Giles, *The Last Kaiser – The Life of Wilhelm II*, St. Martin's Press, New York, 2000 p.430

28. Ilsemann, von, Sigurd, *Wilhelm II in Nederland 1918 – 1941*, Uitgeverij Aspekt, Soesterberg, 2015 p.175

29. *Ibid.*

30. MacDonogh, Giles, *The Last Kaiser – The Life of Wilhelm II*, St. Martin's Press, New York, 2000 p.430

31. Herzogin zu Braunschweig und Lüneburg, Viktoria Luise, *The Kaiser's Daughter – Memoirs of H.R.H. Viktoria Luise, Duchess of Brunswick and Lüneburg, Princess of Prussia*, W.H. Allen, London, 1977 p.159

32. Röhl, John C.G., *Wilhelm II – Into the Abyss of War and Exile 1900-1941*, Cambridge University Press, Cambridge, 2015 p.1211

33. Herzogin zu Braunschweig und Lüneburg, Viktoria Luise, *The Kaiser's Daughter – Memoirs of H.R.H. Viktoria Luise, Duchess of Brunswick and Lüneburg, Princess of Prussia*, W.H. Allen, London, 1977 p.159

34. Ilsemann, von, Sigurd, *Wilhelm II in Nederland 1918 – 1941*, Uitgeverij Aspekt, Soesterberg, 2015 p.176

35. Herzogin zu Braunschweig und Lüneburg, Viktoria Luise, *The Kaiser's Daughter – Memoirs of H.R.H. Viktoria Luise, Duchess of Brunswick and Lüneburg, Princess of Prussia*, W.H. Allen, London, 1977 p.160

36. Herzogin zu Braunschweig und Lüneburg, Viktoria Luise, *The Kaiser's Daughter – Memoirs of H.R.H. Viktoria Luise, Duchess of Brunswick and Lüneburg, Princess of Prussia*, W.H. Allen, London, 1977 p.160-161

37. Ilsemann, von, Sigurd, *Wilhelm II in Nederland 1918 – 1941*, Uitgeverij Aspekt, Soesterberg, 2015 p.178

38. Röhl, John C.G., *Wilhelm II – Into the Abyss of War and Exile 1900-1941*, Cambridge University Press, Cambridge, 2015 p.1210

39. The New York Times (19 September 1922) *Ex-Kaiser shocks German Royalists*

40. Empress Hermine, *Days in Doorn*, Hutchinson, London,

1928 p.XXXIV-XXXV

41. Empress Hermine, *Days in Doorn*, Hutchinson, London, 1928 p.177-178

42. Waite, Robert G.L., *Kaiser and Führer: A Comparative Study of Personality and Politics*, University of Toronto Press, Toronto, 1998 p.21

43. Empress Hermine, *Days in Doorn*, Hutchinson, London, 1928 p.XIX-XX

44. Empress Hermine, *Days in Doorn*, Hutchinson, London, 1928 p.XXXV

45. Waite, Robert G.L., *Kaiser and Führer: A Comparative Study of Personality and Politics*, University of Toronto Press, Toronto, 1998 p.27

46. Waite, Robert G.L., *Kaiser and Führer: A Comparative Study of Personality and Politics*, University of Toronto Press, Toronto, 1998 p.26

47. *Ibid.*

48. MacDonogh, Giles, *The Last Kaiser – The Life of Wilhelm II*, St. Martin's Press, New York, 2000 p.430

49. Ilsemann, von, Sigurd, *Wilhelm II in Nederland 1918 – 1941*, Uitgeverij Aspekt, Soesterberg, 2015 p.195

50. Herzogin zu Braunschweig und Lüneburg, Viktoria Luise, *The Kaiser's Daughter – Memoirs of H.R.H. Viktoria Luise, Duchess of Brunswick and Lüneburg, Princess of Prussia*, W.H. Allen, London, 1977 p.161-162

51. Herzogin zu Braunschweig und Lüneburg, Viktoria Luise, *The Kaiser's Daughter – Memoirs of H.R.H. Viktoria Luise, Duchess of Brunswick and Lüneburg, Princess of Prussia*, W.H. Allen, London, 1977 p.162

52. Ilsemann, von, Sigurd, *Wilhelm II in Nederland 1918 – 1941*, Uitgeverij Aspekt, Soesterberg, 2015 p.192

53. The New York Times (6 November 1922) *Ex-Kaiser married at House of Doorn*

54. Röhl, John C.G., *Wilhelm II – Into the Abyss of War and Exile*

1900-1941, Cambridge University Press, Cambridge, 2015 p.1211

55. The New York Time (3 November 1922) *Dutch Customs Men Hold Hermine's Bridal Dresses*

56. MacDonogh, Giles, *The Last Kaiser – The Life of Wilhelm II*, St. Martin's Press, New York, 2000 p.434

57. Toom, den, Friedhild & Klein, Sven Michael, Hermine – *Die zweite Gemahlin von Wilhelm II*, Verein für Greizer Geschichte, Greiz, 2007 p.57

58. Empress Hermine, *Days in Doorn*, Hutchinson, London, 1928 p.XV

59. Ilsemann, von, Sigurd, *Wilhelm II in Nederland 1918 – 1941*, Uitgeverij Aspekt, Soesterberg, 2015 p.196

60. The New York Times (6 November 1922) *Ex-Kaiser married at House of Doorn*

61. The New York Times (21 November 1922) *Ex-Kaiser bestows forbidden decoration*

62. Voorwaarts : sociaal-democratisch dagblad (15 November 1922) *Het diadeem der keizerin*

63. Empress Hermine, *Days in Doorn*, Hutchinson, London, 1928 p.95

64. Herzogin zu Braunschweig und Lüneburg, Viktoria Luise, *The Kaiser's Daughter – Memoirs of H.R.H. Viktoria Luise, Duchess of Brunswick and Lüneburg, Princess of Prussia*, W.H. Allen, London, 1977 p.164

Chapter 5

1. Trouw (20-12-1978) *De Huisdienaar van de Keizer*

2. Empress Hermine, *Days in Doorn*, Hutchinson, London, 1928 p.XXIII

3. Ilsemann, von, Sigurd, *Wilhelm II in Nederland 1918 – 1941*, Uitgeverij Aspekt, Soesterberg, 2015 p.200

4. Empress Hermine, *Days in Doorn*, Hutchinson, London, 1928 p. XXIV

5. Ilsemann, von, Sigurd, *Wilhelm II in Nederland 1918 – 1941*, Uitgeverij Aspekt, Soesterberg, 2015 p.202

6. Ilsemann, von, Sigurd, *Wilhelm II in Nederland 1918 – 1941*, Uitgeverij Aspekt, Soesterberg, 2015 p.208

7. Ilsemann, von, Sigurd, *Wilhelm II in Nederland 1918 – 1941*, Uitgeverij Aspekt, Soesterberg, 2015 p.212

8. De Indische courant 05-09-1923 *Een Interview met Keizerin Hermine*

9. Ilsemann, von, Sigurd, *Wilhelm II in Nederland 1918 – 1941*, Uitgeverij Aspekt, Soesterberg, 2015 p.215

10. Ilsemann, von, Sigurd, *Wilhelm II in Nederland 1918 – 1941*, Uitgeverij Aspekt, Soesterberg, 2015 p.229

11. Ilsemann, von, Sigurd, *Wilhelm II in Nederland 1918 – 1941*, Uitgeverij Aspekt, Soesterberg, 2015 p.218

12. MacDonogh, Giles, *The Last Kaiser – The Life of Wilhelm II*, St. Martin's Press, New York, 2000 p.435

13. Röhl, John C.G., *Wilhelm II – Into the Abyss of War and Exile 1900-1941*, Cambridge University Press, Cambridge, 2015 p.1212

14. *Ibid.*

15. Ilsemann, von, Sigurd, *Wilhelm II in Nederland 1918 – 1941*, Uitgeverij Aspekt, Soesterberg, 2015 p.220

16. Ilsemann, von, Sigurd, *Wilhelm II in Nederland 1918 – 1941*, Uitgeverij Aspekt, Soesterberg, 2015 p.221

17. The New York Times (13 June 1924) *Hermine is very ill; ex-Kaiser is worried*

18. The New York Times (30 July 1924) *Ex-Kaiser's wife seeks treatment*

19. Toom, den, Friedhild & Klein, Sven Michael, Hermine – *Die zweite Gemahlin von Wilhelm II*, Verein für Greizer Geschichte, Greiz, 2007 p.62

20. The New York Times (7 March 1923) *Hermine plans trip home*

21. The New York Times (12 July 1925) *The Ex-Kaiser speaks his mind*

22. Empress Hermine, *Days in Doorn*, Hutchinson, London, 1928 p.XXIV

23. Empress Hermine, *Days in Doorn*, Hutchinson, London, 1928 p.XXVII

24. Empress Hermine, *Days in Doorn*, Hutchinson, London, 1928 p.260-261

25. Ilsemann, von, Sigurd, *Wilhelm II in Nederland 1918 – 1941*, Uitgeverij Aspekt, Soesterberg, 2015 p.242

26. Ilsemann, von, Sigurd, *Wilhelm II in Nederland 1918 – 1941*, Uitgeverij Aspekt, Soesterberg, 2015 p.243

27. Ilsemann, von, Sigurd, *Wilhelm II in Nederland 1918 – 1941*, Uitgeverij Aspekt, Soesterberg, 2015 p.244

28. *Ibid.*

29. Ilsemann, von, Sigurd, *Wilhelm II in Nederland 1918 – 1941*, Uitgeverij Aspekt, Soesterberg, 2015 p.246

30. De Maasbode 13-03-1925 *De echtgenoote van den voormaligen Duitschen keizer*

31. De Grondwet 13-03-1925 *In enkele regels*

32. Nieuwsblad van het Noorden 02-04-1925 *Gemengde berichten*

33. Ilsemann, von, Sigurd, *Wilhelm II in Nederland 1918 – 1941*, Uitgeverij Aspekt, Soesterberg, 2015 p.252

34. The New York Times (31 May 1925) *Ex-Kaiser visits dowager Queen*

35. De Grondwet (07-07-1925) *Een ex-keizerlijk uitstapje naar Middachten*

36. The New York Times (22 November 1925) *Demand prosecution of ex-Kaiser's wife*

37. Ilsemann, von, Sigurd, *Wilhelm II in Nederland 1918 – 1941*, Uitgeverij Aspekt, Soesterberg, 2015 p.261

38. Ilsemann, von, Sigurd, *Wilhelm II in Nederland 1918 – 1941*, Uitgeverij Aspekt, Soesterberg, 2015 p.264

39. Haagsche courant (26-08-1926) *Een eisch tegen de echtgenoote van den ex-keizer*

40. Het Vaderland : staat- en letterkundig nieuwsblad (10-11-

1927) *De ex-keizer wint een proces*

41. Ilsemann, von, Sigurd, *Wilhelm II in Nederland 1918 – 1941*, Uitgeverij Aspekt, Soesterberg, 2015 p.280

42. Empress Hermine, *Days in Doorn*, Hutchinson, London, 1928 p.104

43. The New York Times (2 November 1927) *Cycle crash kills stepson of ex-Kaiser*

44. De Maasbode 06-11-1927 *Laatste berichten*

45. The New York Times (15 October 1927) *Prince of Reuss dies*

46. De Grondwet 14-10-1927 *Kort gemengd nieuws*

47. Ilsemann, von, Sigurd, *Wilhelm II in Nederland 1918 – 1941*, Uitgeverij Aspekt, Soesterberg, 2015 p.311

48. Ilsemann, von, Sigurd, *Wilhelm II in Nederland 1918 – 1941*, Uitgeverij Aspekt, Soesterberg, 2015 p.331

49. Ilsemann, von, Sigurd, *Wilhelm II in Nederland 1918 – 1941*, Uitgeverij Aspekt, Soesterberg, 2015 p.332

50. MacDonogh, Giles, *The Last Kaiser – The Life of Wilhelm II*, St. Martin's Press, New York, 2000 p.444

51. Twentsch dagblad Tubantia en Enschedesche courant (28-01-1929) *De 70e verjaardag van ex-keizer Wilhelm*

52. Nieuwe Tilburgsche Courant (17-04-1929) *De oplichter Hartung*

53. Haagsche courant (25-05-1929) *Navolger van Domela*

54. Limburger koerier : provinciaal dagblad (10-08-1929) *Het Proces Karl Hartung*

55. De Telegraaf (04-12-1929) *Oplichter Hartung weer voor de rechtbank*

56. Haagsche courant (08-09-1933) *De "koerier des keizers"*

57. Koninklijk Huisarchief A47 - *Letter 4 January 1930*

58. De Gooi- en Eemlander : nieuws- en advertentieblad (10-06-1930) *Feest op Huize Doorn*

59. Delftsche courant (19-06-1930) *Ernstig ongeluk op de Kager Plassen*

60. Ilsemann, von, Sigurd, *Wilhelm II in Nederland 1918 – 1941*,

Uitgeverij Aspekt, Soesterberg, 2015 p.344-345

61. Ilsemann, von, Sigurd, *Wilhelm II in Nederland 1918 – 1941*, Uitgeverij Aspekt, Soesterberg, 2015 p.351

62. Toom, den, Friedhild & Klein, Sven Michael, Hermine – *Die zweite Gemahlin von Wilhelm II*, Verein für Greizer Geschichte, Greiz, 2007 p.78

63. Toom, den, Friedhild & Klein, Sven Michael, Hermine – *Die zweite Gemahlin von Wilhelm II*, Verein für Greizer Geschichte, Greiz, 2007 p.78-79

64. Petropoulos, Jonathan, *Royals and the Reich*, Oxford University Press, Oxford, 2006 p.104

65. Ilsemann, von, Sigurd, *Wilhelm II in Nederland 1918 – 1941*, Uitgeverij Aspekt, Soesterberg, 2015 p.360

66. Ilsemann, von, Sigurd, *Wilhelm II in Nederland 1918 – 1941*, Uitgeverij Aspekt, Soesterberg, 2015 p.361

67. MacDonogh, Giles, *The Last Kaiser – The Life of Wilhelm II*, St. Martin's Press, New York, 2000 p.447

68. MacDonogh, Giles, *The Last Kaiser – The Life of Wilhelm II*, St. Martin's Press, New York, 2000 p.446

69. Herzogin zu Braunschweig und Lüneburg, Viktoria Luise, *The Kaiser's Daughter – Memoirs of H.R.H. Viktoria Luise, Duchess of Brunswick and Lüneburg, Princess of Prussia*, W.H. Allen, London, 1977 p.173

70. Ilsemann, von, Sigurd, *Wilhelm II in Nederland 1918 – 1941*, Uitgeverij Aspekt, Soesterberg, 2015 p.362

71. MacDonogh, Giles, *The Last Kaiser – The Life of Wilhelm II*, St. Martin's Press, New York, 2000 p.447

72. Ilsemann, von, Sigurd, *Wilhelm II in Nederland 1918 – 1941*, Uitgeverij Aspekt, Soesterberg, 2015 p.372-373

73. Ilsemann, von, Sigurd, *Wilhelm II in Nederland 1918 – 1941*, Uitgeverij Aspekt, Soesterberg, 2015 p.371-372

74. Ilsemann, von, Sigurd, *Wilhelm II in Nederland 1918 – 1941*, Uitgeverij Aspekt, Soesterberg, 2015 p.372

75. Nieuwsblad van het Noorden (21-11-1931) *Prinses Hermine*

in Berlijn

76. Petropoulos, Jonathan, *Royals and the Reich*, Oxford University Press, Oxford, 2006 p.102

77. Röhl, John C.G., *Wilhelm II – Into the Abyss of War and Exile 1900-1941*, Cambridge University Press, Cambridge, 2015 p.1247

78. Ilsemann, von, Sigurd, *Wilhelm II in Nederland 1918 – 1941*, Uitgeverij Aspekt, Soesterberg, 2015 p.406

79. Ilsemann, von, Sigurd, *Wilhelm II in Nederland 1918 – 1941*, Uitgeverij Aspekt, Soesterberg, 2015 p.409

80. Het volk : dagblad voor de arbeiderspartij (6 September 1932) *Koningin-moeder bezoekt ex-keizer*

81. Limburger koerier (6 September 1932) *Wilhelm naar Zandvoort*

82. MacDonogh, Giles, *The Last Kaiser – The Life of Wilhelm II*, St. Martin's Press, New York, 2000 p.54

83. Fromm, Bella, *Blood & Banquets: A Berlin Diary 1930 – 1938*, Simon & Schuster, New York, 1990 p.58

84. Fromm, Bella, *Blood & Banquets: A Berlin Diary 1930 – 1938*, Simon & Schuster, New York, 1990 p.62

85. MacDonogh, Giles, *The Last Kaiser – The Life of Wilhelm II*, St. Martin's Press, New York, 2000 p.449

86. De Sumatra post (24-12-1932) *De mislukte aanslag op Huize Doorn*

87. Bataviaasch nieuwsblad (20-02-1933) *Doorn in het oog der Franschen*

88. Scheel, Klaus, *1933 – Der Tag von Potsdam*, Brandenburghisches Verlagshaus, Berlin, 1996 p.71-72

89. De Tijd : godsdienstig-staatkundig dagblad (25-02-1933) *Hitler en de monarchie*

90. Ilsemann, von, Sigurd, *Wilhelm II in Nederland 1918 – 1941*, Uitgeverij Aspekt, Soesterberg, 2015 p.417

91. Fromm, Bella, *Blood & Banquets: A Berlin Diary 1930 – 1938*, Simon & Schuster, New York, 1990 p.109

92. Ilsemann, von, Sigurd, *Wilhelm II in Nederland 1918 – 1941*, Uitgeverij Aspekt, Soesterberg, 2015 p.421

93. Ilsemann, von, Sigurd, *Wilhelm II in Nederland 1918 – 1941*, Uitgeverij Aspekt, Soesterberg, 2015 p.420

94. Ilsemann, von, Sigurd, *Wilhelm II in Nederland 1918 – 1941*, Uitgeverij Aspekt, Soesterberg, 2015 p.425

95. Ilsemann, von, Sigurd, *Wilhelm II in Nederland 1918 – 1941*, Uitgeverij Aspekt, Soesterberg, 2015 p.428

96. Ilsemann, von, Sigurd, *Wilhelm II in Nederland 1918 – 1941*, Uitgeverij Aspekt, Soesterberg, 2015 p.430

97. Petropoulos, Jonathan, *Royals and the Reich*, Oxford University Press, Oxford, 2006 p.104-105

98. Petropoulos, Jonathan, *Royals and the Reich*, Oxford University Press, Oxford, 2006 p.108

99. Petropoulos, Jonathan, *Royals and the Reich*, Oxford University Press, Oxford, 2006 p.108-109

100. Petropoulos, Jonathan, *Royals and the Reich*, Oxford University Press, Oxford, 2006 p.154

101. *Ibid.*

102. Petropoulos, Jonathan, *Royals and the Reich*, Oxford University Press, Oxford, 2006 p.162

103. Herzogin zu Braunschweig und Lüneburg, Viktoria Luise, *The Kaiser's Daughter – Memoirs of H.R.H. Viktoria Luise, Duchess of Brunswick and Lüneburg, Princess of Prussia*, W.H. Allen, London, 1977 p.179

104. Herzogin zu Braunschweig und Lüneburg, Viktoria Luise, *The Kaiser's Daughter – Memoirs of H.R.H. Viktoria Luise, Duchess of Brunswick and Lüneburg, Princess of Prussia*, W.H. Allen, London, 1977 p.88

105. Ilsemann, von, Sigurd, *Wilhelm II in Nederland 1918 – 1941*, Uitgeverij Aspekt, Soesterberg, 2015 p.437

106. Ilsemann, von, Sigurd, *Wilhelm II in Nederland 1918 – 1941*, Uitgeverij Aspekt, Soesterberg, 2015 p.439

107. Ilsemann, von, Sigurd, *Wilhelm II in Nederland 1918 – 1941*,

Uitgeverij Aspekt, Soesterberg, 2015 p.442

108. Het volk : dagblad voor de arbeiderspartij (26-01-1934) *Ex-keizer vijf en zeventig*

109. Petropoulos, Jonathan, *Royals and the Reich*, Oxford University Press, Oxford, 2006 p.109

110. *Ibid.*

111. Ilsemann, von, Sigurd, *Wilhelm II in Nederland 1918 – 1941*, Uitgeverij Aspekt, Soesterberg, 2015 p.443

112. Ilsemann, von, Sigurd, *Wilhelm II in Nederland 1918 – 1941*, Uitgeverij Aspekt, Soesterberg, 2015 p.444

113. Ilsemann, von, Sigurd, *Wilhelm II in Nederland 1918 – 1941*, Uitgeverij Aspekt, Soesterberg, 2015 p.448

114. *Ibid.*

115. Röhl, John C.G., *Wilhelm II – Into the Abyss of War and Exile 1900-1941*, Cambridge University Press, Cambridge, 2015 p.1256

116. Ilsemann, von, Sigurd, *Wilhelm II in Nederland 1918 – 1941*, Uitgeverij Aspekt, Soesterberg, 2015 p.452

117. Ilsemann, von, Sigurd, *Wilhelm II in Nederland 1918 – 1941*, Uitgeverij Aspekt, Soesterberg, 2015 p.462

118. Limburgsch dagblad (16-03-1934) *De financieele moeilijkheden op Huize Doorn*

119. Limburger koerier : provinciaal dagblad (05-11-1934) *Hooge belangstelling voor poppententoonstelling*

120. Haagsche courant (07-12-1934) *De echtgenoote van den ex-keizer opent bazar in Berlijn*

121. Nieuwsblad van het Noorden (17-12-1934) *De nat.-soc pers spot met Prinses Hermine, de echtgenoote van den ex-keizer*

122. Het Vaderland : staat- en letterkundig nieuwsblad (20-03-1935) *Herdenking van H.M. De Koningin-Moeder*

123. Withuis, Jolande, *Juliana, Vorstin in een mannenwereld*, De Bezige Bij, Amsterdam, 2016 p.68

124. Zijl, van der, Annejet, *Bernhard – Een verborgen geschiedenis*, Uitgeverij Querido, Amsterdam, 2010 p.237

125. Fasseur, Cees, *Juliana & Bernhard : het verhaal van een huwelijk ; de jaren 1936-1956*, Uitgeverij Balans, Amsterdam, 2008 p.37

126. De Tijd : godsdienstig-staatkundig dagblad (30-06-1938) *Ex-keizer op Soestdijk*

127. Fasseur, Cees, *Juliana & Bernhard : het verhaal van een huwelijk ; de jaren 1936-1956*, Uitgeverij Balans, Amsterdam, 2008 p.76

128. Provinciale Overijsselsche en Zwolsche courant (31-01-1935) *Aanslag op ex-keizer*

129. Nieuwsblad van het Noorden (20-07-1935) *Een verloving te Doorn?*

130. Fromm, Bella, *Blood & Banquets: A Berlin Diary 1930 – 1938*, Simon & Schuster, New York, 1990 p.211-212

131. Röhl, John C.G., *Wilhelm II – Into the Abyss of War and Exile 1900-1941*, Cambridge University Press, Cambridge, 2015 p.1256

132. *Ibid.*

133. Röhl, John C.G., *Wilhelm II – Into the Abyss of War and Exile 1900-1941*, Cambridge University Press, Cambridge, 2015 p.1257

134. *Ibid*

135. Ilsemann, von, Sigurd, *Wilhelm II in Nederland 1918 – 1941*, Uitgeverij Aspekt, Soesterberg, 2015 p.473

136. Ilsemann, von, Sigurd, *Wilhelm II in Nederland 1918 – 1941*, Uitgeverij Aspekt, Soesterberg, 2015 p.478

137. Haagsche courant (11-12-1936) *Stiefdochter van den ex-keizer in het huwelijk getreden*

138. The New York Times (11 December 1936) *Commoner is wed to Princess Carmo*

139. Kern, Gary, *A Death in Washington*, Enigma Books, New York, 2003 p. 113

140. Fromm, Bella, *Blood & Banquets: A Berlin Diary 1930 – 1938*, Simon & Schuster, New York, 1990 p.243

141. Twentsch dagblad Tubantia en Enschedesche courant (10-08-1937) *Ex-keixer Wilhelm II bezoekt het kasteel Twickel te Delden*

142. The New York Times (27 October 1937) *Ex-Kaiser's wife home again*

143. The New York Times (11 December 1936) *Commoner is wed to Princess Carmo*

144. De Grondwet (21-09-1937) *Vrouw hersteld*

145. Nieuwe Tilburgsche Courant (30-12-1937) *De verloving op Huize Doorn*

146. Friesch dagblad (31-01-1938) *Vreugde op Doorn House*

147. Ilsemann, von, Sigurd, *Wilhelm II in Nederland 1918 – 1941*, Uitgeverij Aspekt, Soesterberg, 2015 p.485

148. Röhl, John C.G., *Wilhelm II – Into the Abyss of War and Exile 1900-1941*, Cambridge University Press, Cambridge, 2015 p.1258

149. De Telegraaf (28-02-1938) *Prinses Hermine naar Beieren*

150. Haagsche courant (28-04-1938) *De ex-keizer van Duitschland*

151. Fromm, Bella, *Blood & Banquets: A Berlin Diary 1930 – 1938*, Simon & Schuster, New York, 1990 p.263

152. The New York Times (3 May 1938) *Ferdinand and Kira to wed again today*

153. Algemeen Handelsblad (24-07-1938) *Prinses Hermine te Utrecht*

154. Leeuwarder nieuwsblad (18-08-1938) *Vroegere glorie herleefd*

155. Het Vaderland : staat- en letterkundig nieuwsblad (26-09-1938) *De ex-keizer te Amsterdam*

156. De Gooi- en Eemlander : nieuws- en advertentieblad (12-10-1938) *Prinses Hermine terug uit Duitschland*

157. De Telegraaf (26-11-1938) *Prinses Hermine en Duitsche Kroonprins vertrekken*

158. De Tijd : godsdienstig-staatkundig dagblad (26-01-1939) *Vijftigtal gasten op Huize Doorn*

159. Bredasche courant (30-01-1939) *Aanbieding van een*

verjaardagsgeschenk aan den Duitschen ex-keizer

160. Herzogin zu Braunschweig und Lüneburg, Viktoria Luise, *The Kaiser's Daughter – Memoirs of H.R.H. Viktoria Luise, Duchess of Brunswick and Lüneburg, Princess of Prussia*, W.H. Allen, London, 1977 p.193

161. Herzogin zu Braunschweig und Lüneburg, Viktoria Luise, *The Kaiser's Daughter – Memoirs of H.R.H. Viktoria Luise, Duchess of Brunswick and Lüneburg, Princess of Prussia*, W.H. Allen, London, 1977 p.196

162. Ilsemann, von, Sigurd, *Wilhelm II in Nederland 1918 – 1941*, Uitgeverij Aspekt, Soesterberg, 2015 p.507

163. Algemeen Handelsblad (15-04-1939) *Kleinzoon van ex-keizer op Huize Doorn*

164. Algemeen Handelsblad (28-04-1939) *Prinselijk paar bij den ex-keizer*

165. De Telegraaf (09-05-1939) *Stiefzoon van den ex-keizer verloofd*

166. De Telegraaf (07-06-1939) *Prinses Hermine – Vrouw van een ex-keizer*

167. Röhl, John C.G., *Wilhelm II – Into the Abyss of War and Exile 1900-1941*, Cambridge University Press, Cambridge, 2015 p.1259

168. Röhl, John C.G., *Wilhelm II – Into the Abyss of War and Exile 1900-1941*, Cambridge University Press, Cambridge, 2015 p.1260

169. *Ibid*

170. Nieuwe Apeldoornsche courant (10-01-1940) *Graaf Bentinck bijgezet*

171. Nieuwe Tilburgsche Courant (29-01-1940) *Stille verjaardag te Doorn*

172. Ilsemann, von, Sigurd, *Wilhelm II in Nederland 1918 – 1941*, Uitgeverij Aspekt, Soesterberg, 2015 p.520

173. MacDonogh, Giles, *The Last Kaiser – The Life of Wilhelm II*, St. Martin's Press, New York, 2000 p.458

174. Ilsemann, von, Sigurd, *Wilhelm II in Nederland 1918 – 1941*,

Uitgeverij Aspekt, Soesterberg, 2015 p.520

175. MacDonogh, Giles, *The Last Kaiser – The Life of Wilhelm II*, St. Martin's Press, New York, 2000 p.458

176. *Ibid.*

177. Herzogin zu Braunschweig und Lüneburg, Viktoria Luise, *The Kaiser's Daughter – Memoirs of H.R.H. Viktoria Luise, Duchess of Brunswick and Lüneburg, Princess of Prussia*, W.H. Allen, London, 1977 p.204

178. Herzogin zu Braunschweig und Lüneburg, Viktoria Luise, *The Kaiser's Daughter – Memoirs of H.R.H. Viktoria Luise, Duchess of Brunswick and Lüneburg, Princess of Prussia*, W.H. Allen, London, 1977 p.203

179. Röhl, John C.G., *Wilhelm II – Into the Abyss of War and Exile 1900-1941*, Cambridge University Press, Cambridge, 2015 p.1260-1261

180. Röhl, John C.G., *Wilhelm II – Into the Abyss of War and Exile 1900-1941*, Cambridge University Press, Cambridge, 2015 p.1260

181. MacDonogh, Giles, *The Last Kaiser – The Life of Wilhelm II*, St. Martin's Press, New York, 2000 p.458

182. Toom, den, Friedhild & Klein, Sven Michael, *Hermine – Die zweite Gemahlin von Wilhelm II*, Verein für Greizer Geschichte, Greiz, 2007 p.85

183. Ilsemann, von, Sigurd, *Wilhelm II in Nederland 1918 – 1941*, Uitgeverij Aspekt, Soesterberg, 2015 p.524

184. Het dagblad : uitgave van de Nederlandsche Dagbladpers te Batavia (16-11-1948) *"Keizerin" Hermine deed als Wilhelm en zond Hitler gelukswensen*

185. The New York Times (7 August 1940) *Ex-Kaiser's stepdaughter to marry his grandson*

186. The New York Times (2 October 1940) *German prince married*

187. Herzogin zu Braunschweig und Lüneburg, Viktoria Luise, *The Kaiser's Daughter – Memoirs of H.R.H. Viktoria Luise, Duchess of Brunswick and Lüneburg, Princess of Prussia*, W.H.

Allen, London, 1977 p.207-208

188. MacDonogh, Giles, *The Last Kaiser – The Life of Wilhelm II*, St. Martin's Press, New York, 2000 p.459

189. Ilsemann, von, Sigurd, *Wilhelm II in Nederland 1918 – 1941*, Uitgeverij Aspekt, Soesterberg, 2015 p.526

190. Trouw (20-12-1978) *De Huisdienaar van de Keizer*

191. Herzogin zu Braunschweig und Lüneburg, Viktoria Luise, *The Kaiser's Daughter – Memoirs of H.R.H. Viktoria Luise, Duchess of Brunswick and Lüneburg, Princess of Prussia*, W.H. Allen, London, 1977 p.208

192. Herzogin zu Braunschweig und Lüneburg, Viktoria Luise, *The Kaiser's Daughter – Memoirs of H.R.H. Viktoria Luise, Duchess of Brunswick and Lüneburg, Princess of Prussia*, W.H. Allen, London, 1977 p.177-178

193. Herzogin zu Braunschweig und Lüneburg, Viktoria Luise, *The Kaiser's Daughter – Memoirs of H.R.H. Viktoria Luise, Duchess of Brunswick and Lüneburg, Princess of Prussia*, W.H. Allen, London, 1977 p.209

Chapter 6

1. Waite, Robert G.L., *Kaiser and Führer: A Comparative Study of Personality and Politics*, University of Toronto Press, Toronto, 1998 p.360

2. Ven, Van der, F.A.J. (2001) Huis Doorn: een hoofdstuk uit de Nederlandse geschiedenis. Rechtsgeleerd magazijn Thema, 67-81

3. Serrien, Pieter, *Het elfde uur: 11 november 1918, de gewelddadige laatste dag van de Eerste Wereldoorlog*, Horizon, Antwerpen, 2018 p.401

4. Toom, den, Friedhild & Klein, Sven Michael, Hermine – *Die zweite Gemahlin von Wilhelm II*, Verein für Greizer Geschichte, Greiz, 2007 p.90

5. *Ibid.*

6. The New York Times (29 August 1943) *Ex-Kaiser's stepson*

killed

7.   Nationaal Archief – *Collectie J.B. Kan Inv 3 18 December 1943*

8.   Toom, den, Friedhild & Klein, Sven Michael, Hermine – *Die zweite Gemahlin von Wilhelm II*, Verein für Greizer Geschichte, Greiz, 2007 p.90

9.   Herzogin zu Braunschweig und Lüneburg, Viktoria Luise, *The Kaiser's Daughter – Memoirs of H.R.H. Viktoria Luise, Duchess of Brunswick and Lüneburg, Princess of Prussia*, W.H. Allen, London, 1977 p.229

10. Toom, den, Friedhild & Klein, Sven Michael, Hermine – *Die zweite Gemahlin von Wilhelm II*, Verein für Greizer Geschichte, Greiz, 2007 p.91

11. Petropoulos, Jonathan, *Royals and the Reich*, Oxford University Press, Oxford, 2006 p.164-165

12. Petropoulos, Jonathan, *Royals and the Reich*, Oxford University Press, Oxford, 2006 p.165-166

13. United States Holocaust Memorial Museum Collection, Gift of Howard S. Sichel and Linda Sichel Strohmenger – *Letter dated 28 April 1945 from Letters Home, Highlights, 1943-1946*

14. Daily News (New York, New York - 17 April 1945) *Kaiser's Captive Widow Mourns Old Reich*

15. MacDonogh, Giles, *The Last Kaiser – The Life of Wilhelm II*, St. Martin's Press, New York, 2000 p.297

16. Petropoulos, Jonathan, *Royals and the Reich*, Oxford University Press, Oxford, 2006 p.468n 49

17. The New York Times (4 February 1947) *Kaiser's widow robbed*

18. Nieuwsblad van het Zuiden : dagblad met ochtend- en avond-editie (17-04-1947) *De weduwe van des eens machtigen keizer*

19. Leeuwarder courant : hoofdblad van Friesland (22-04-1947) *Prinses Hermine heeft nog twee tafels en een stoel*

20. Pierik, Perry & Pors, Henk, *De verlaten monarch*, Uitgeverij Aspekt, Soesterberg, 2012, p.170

21. The Times-Tribune (21 August 1947) *Widow of Kaiser*

disturbed by Red Police Supervision

22. The New York Times (10 August 1947) *Prince implies Soviet link in theft of German gems*

23. The New York Times (10 August 1947) *Soviet link seen in German theft*

24. The New York Times (10 August 1947) *Poison suspected in Hermine death*

25. Die Welt (12 August 1947) *Kronjuwelenaffäre noch ungeklärt*

26. The New York Times (11 August 1947) *Hermine gem case dropped by army*

27. Algemeen Handelsblad (16 August 1947) *Prinses Hermine te Potsdam begraven*

28. Pierik, Perry & Pors, Henk, *De verlaten monarch*, Uitgeverij Aspekt, Soesterberg, 2012, p.171

29. Pors, Henk, *De ondergang van Kaiserin Hermine*, Pors, Capelle aan den IJssel, 1995, p.10-11

30. Pors, Henk, *De ondergang van Kaiserin Hermine*, Pors, Capelle aan den IJssel, 1995, p.12

31. The New York Times (25 October 1947) *German Prince wins appeal*

32. The New York Times (14 September 1947) *German gems divided*

33. Nationaal Archief Den Haag - Nederlandse Ambassade in de Bondsrepubliek Duitsland te Bonn en de Nederlandse Militaire Missie bij de Geallieerde Bestuursraad Berlijn – *14 May 1948 Inv. 468*

34. Nationaal Archief Den Haag - Nederlandse Ambassade in de Bondsrepubliek Duitsland te Bonn en de Nederlandse Militaire Missie bij de Geallieerde Bestuursraad Berlijn – *2 November 1948 Inv. 468*

35. Urbach, Karina, *Go-Betweens for Hitler*, Oxford University Press, Oxford, 2015 p.233

References

Books and articles

Scheel, Klaus, *1933 – Der Tag von Potsdam*, Brandenburghisches Verlagshaus, Berlin, 1996

Empress Hermine, *Days in Doorn*, Hutchinson, London, 1928

Fasseur, Cees, *Juliana & Bernhard : het verhaal van een huwelijk ; de jaren 1936-1956*, Uitgeverij Balans, Amsterdam, 2008

Fasseur, Cees, *Wilhelmina – De jonge koningin*, Uitgeverij Balans, Amsterdam, 1998

Fromm, Bella, *Blood & Banquets: A Berlin Diary 1930 – 1938*, Simon & Schuster, New York, 1990

Fulford, Roger (edited), *Dearest Child – Letters between Queen Victoria and the Princess Royal*, Holt, Rinehart and Winston, New York, 1964 p.159

Graaf, de, Beatrice, *Vorstin op vredespad*, Tijdschrift voor Geschiedenis v131 n4, 2018

Herzogin zu Braunschweig und Lüneburg, Viktoria Luise, *The Kaiser's Daughter – Memoirs of H.R.H. Viktoria Luise, Duchess of Brunswick and Lüneburg, Princess of Prussia*, W.H. Allen, London, 1977

Ilsemann, von, Sigurd, *Wilhelm II in Nederland 1918 – 1941*, Uitgeverij Aspekt, Soesterberg, 2015

Kern, Gary, *A Death in Washington*, Enigma Books, New York, 2003

Kiste, van der, John, *The last German Empress*, CreateSpace Independent Publishing Platform, Scotts Valley, 2015

MacDonogh, Giles, *The Last Kaiser – The Life of Wilhelm II*, St. Martin's Press, New York, 2000

Mansel, Philip and Riotte, Torsten, *Monarchy and exile: The politics of legitimacy from Marie de Médicis to Wilhelm II*, Palgrave Macmillan, Basingstoke, 2011

Moeyes, Paul, *Het kleine keizersdrama in Amerongen*, Stichting

Kasteel Amerongen, Amerongen, 2018

Petropoulos, Jonathan, *Royals and the Reich*, Oxford University Press, Oxford, 2006

Pierik, Perry & Pors, Henk, *De verlaten monarch*, Uitgeverij Aspekt, Soesterberg, 2012

Pors, Henk, *De ondergang van Kaiserin Hermine*, Pors, Capelle aan den IJssel, 1995

Ramm, Agatha (edited), *Beloved & darling child: last letters between Queen Victoria and her eldest daughter, 1886-1901*, Sutton Publishing, Stroud, 1998

Reibnitz, von, Kurt, *Wilhelm ll. Und Hermine, Geschichte und Kritik von Doorn*, Reissner, Dresden, 1929

Reuss, Hermine, *Mijn leven en hoe ik den keizer trouwde*, Weekblad Het Leven, Amsterdam, ca. 1930

Richards, Stewart, *Curtain down at Her Majesty's*, The History Press, Stroud, 2019

Röhl, John C.G., *Wilhelm II – Into the Abyss of War and Exile 1900-1941*, Cambridge University Press, Cambridge, 2015

Serrien, Pieter, *Het elfde uur: 11 november 1918, de gewelddadige laatste dag van de Eerste Wereldoorlog*, Horizon, Antwerpen, 2018

Toom, den, Friedhild & Klein, Sven Michael, Hermine – *Die zweite Gemahlin von Wilhelm II*, Verein für Greizer Geschichte, Greiz, 2007

Urbach, Karina, *Go-Betweens for Hitler*, Oxford University Press, Oxford, 2015

Ven, Van der, F.A.J. (2001) Huis Doorn: een hoofdstuk uit de Nederlandse geschiedenis. Rechtsgeleerd magazijn Thema

Waite, Robert G.L., *Kaiser and Führer: A Comparative Study of Personality and Politics*, University of Toronto Press, Toronto, 1998

Withuis, Jolande, *Juliana, Vorstin in een mannenwereld*, De Bezige Bij, Amsterdam, 2016

Zijl, van der, Annejet, *Bernhard – Een verborgen geschiedenis*,

Uitgeverij Querido, Amsterdam, 2010

Newspapers

Algemeen Handelsblad

Bataviaasch nieuwsblad

Bredasche courant

Het dagblad : uitgave van de Nederlandsche Dagbladpers te Batavia

Daily News

Delftsche courant

Friesch dagblad

De Gooi- en Eemlander : nieuws- en advertentieblad

De Grondwet

Haagsche courant

De Indische courant

Leeuwarder courant : hoofdblad van Friesland

Leeuwarder nieuwsblad

Limburger koerier : provinciaal dagblad

Limburgsch dagblad

De Maasbode

The New York Times

Nieuwe Apeldoornsche courant

Nieuwe Tilburgsche Courant

Nieuwsblad van het Noorden

Nieuwsblad van het Zuiden

Provinciale Overijsselsche en Zwolsche courant

De Sumatra post

De Telegraaf

De Tijd : godsdienstig-staatkundig dagblad

The Times-Tribune

Twentsch dagblad Tubantia en Enschedesche courant

Trouw

Het Vaderland : staat- en letterkundig nieuwsblad

Het volk : dagblad voor de arbeiderspartij

Voorwaarts : sociaal-democratisch dagblad
Die Welt

Archives

Koninklijk Huisarchief - A47 and A50

Nationaal Archief Den Haag – Collectie J.B. Kan and Nederlandse Ambassade in de Bondsrepubliek Duitsland te Bonn en de Nederlandse Militaire Missie bij de Geallieerde Bestuursraad Berlijn

United States Holocaust Memorial Museum Collection, Gift of Howard S. Sichel and Linda Sichel Strohmenger

Selected index

Chronos Books
HISTORY

Chronos Books is an historical non-fiction imprint. Chronos publishes real history for real people; bringing to life people, places and events in an imaginative, easy-to-digest and accessible way - histories that pass on their stories to a generation of new readers.
If you have enjoyed this book, why not tell other readers by posting a review on your preferred book site.

Recent bestsellers from Chronos Books are:

Lady Katherine Knollys
The Unacknowledged Daughter of King Henry VIII
Sarah-Beth Watkins
A comprehensive account of Katherine Knollys' questionable
paternity, her previously unexplored life in the Tudor court
and her intriguing relationship with Elizabeth I.
Paperback: 978-1-78279-585-8 ebook: 978-1-78279-584-1

Cromwell was Framed
Ireland 1649
Tom Reilly
Revealed: The definitive research that proves the Irish nation
owes Oliver Cromwell a huge posthumous apology for
wrongly convicting him of civilian atrocities in 1649.
Paperback: 978-1-78279-516-2 ebook: 978-1-78279-515-5

Why The CIA Killed JFK and Malcolm X
The Secret Drug Trade in Laos
John Koerner
A new groundbreaking work presenting evidence that the CIA
silenced JFK to protect its secret drug trade in Laos.
Paperback: 978-1-78279-701-2 ebook: 978-1-78279-700-5

The Disappearing Ninth Legion
A Popular History
Mark Olly
The Disappearing Ninth Legion examines hard evidence for the
foundation, development, mysterious disappearance, or possi-
ble continuation of Rome's lost Legion.
Paperback: 978-1-84694-559-5 ebook: 978-1-84694-931-9

Beaten But Not Defeated
Siegfried Moos - A German anti-Nazi who settled in Britain
Merilyn Moos
Siegi Moos, an anti-Nazi and active member of the German
Communist Party, escaped Germany in 1933 and, exiled in
Britain, sought another route to the transformation
of capitalism.
Paperback: 978-1-78279-677-0 ebook: 978-1-78279-676-3

A Schoolboy's Wartime Letters
An evacuee's life in WWII — A Personal Memoir
Geoffrey Iley
A boy writes home during WWII, revealing his own fascinating
story, full of zest for life, information and humour.
Paperback: 978-1-78279-504-9 ebook: 978-1-78279-503-2

The Life & Times of the Real Robyn Hoode
Mark Olly
A journey of discovery. The chronicles of the genuine historical
character, Robyn Hoode, and how he became one of England's
greatest legends.
Paperback: 978-1-78535-059-7 ebook: 978-1-78535-060-3

Readers of ebooks can buy or view any of these bestsellers by clicking on the live link in the title. Most titles are published in paperback and as an ebook. Paperbacks are available in traditional bookshops. Both print and ebook formats are available online.

Find more titles and sign up to our readers' newsletter at
http://www.johnhuntpublishing.com/history-home

Follow us on Facebook at
https://www.facebook.com/ChronosBooks

and Twitter at https://twitter.com/ChronosBooks